GERMAN HOMOSEXUALITY

From Frederick the Great to W.W. II Berlin

This is a revised edition of my book Prussian Homosexuality.

© 2017

cerning the love of his life Thomas Mann wrote: ''I have lived and oved. I knew happiness, held in my arms he I longed for.''
To the author's mind the very aim of life. The *only* aim of life.

''The right of self-determination over body and soul is the most important basis of all freedom.''
Adolf Brand, founder of the very first homosexual magazine *Der Eigene.*

This is Freud's response to a letter from a woman worried about her son:
''Homosexuality is assuredly no advantage, but it is nothing to be ashamed of, no vice, no degradation; it cannot be classified as an illness; we consider it to be a variation of the sexual function. Many highly respectable individuals of ancient and modern times have been homosexuals, several of the greatest men among them. (Plato, Michelangelo, Leonardo da Vinci, etc). It is a great injustice to persecute homosexuality as a crime--and a cruelty, too.''
Sigmund Freud

''I did not fall in love often. I often kept it to myself. It was forbidden, even in America, and one had to be a little careful.''
Golo Mann, Thomas Mann's son, about his own homosexuality, and, alas, even today, 2017, one still has to be a little careful in the States.
Golo Mann

"The degree and kind of a man's sexuality reach up into the ultimate pinnacle of his spirit."
Nietzsche

The readers of *Der Eigene* ''thirst for a revival of the beauty and values of Ancient Greece, corrupted by years of Christian barbarism.''
Der Eigene founder Adolf Brand

''Christianity gave Eros poison to drink. It did not die from it but it degenerated into a vice.''
Nietzsche

My books include: *Christ has his John, I Have My George: The History of English Homosexuality*; *Exploration Giants*; *Renaissance Murders*; *TROY*; *Greek Homosexuality*; *Roman Homosexuality*; *Renaissance Homosexuality*; *ARGO*; *Boarding School Homosexuality*. I live in the South of France.

CONTENTS

INTRODUCTION

PART VIII

INTRODUCTION

Germany could just as well be called Prussia today because Prussia was its heart and mind, a warrior class that ceased to exist in 1947 when the Allied Control Council, the victors of WWII, abolished the entity with a few rapidly penned signatures at the bottom of a document.

But as seen in this book, far more than some hastily scribbled names will be needed to erase the story of the fiercest fighting force since the Spartans, two brother nations in arms, the Spartans who fought to the death so a lover would never be found lacking in courage and loyalty in the eyes of the boy at his side, and the Prussians headed by a man history calls Frederick the Great, one so powerful that Napoleon himself, gazing down at his grave, proclaimed that he would not be there had Frederick lived, Frederick whose love for men and boys was shared by many of his Prussian soldiers and Prussian compatriots.

The most tolerant gay-friendly nation in the world is, of course, America, San Francisco its Holy Land, but Berlin comes in a clear second today, a capital that celebrates the gay-way every June in a march called Christopher Street Day in remembrance of the Stonewall Revolt. And throughout history, excluding the hellish interval of the Nazi maelstrom, Prussia has been tolerant of homosexuals, the word itself invented in 1869 by Karl-Maria Kertbeny in Vienna and publically defended for the first time in 1867 by the jurist Karl Heinrich Ulrichs in Munich. In 1897 Magnus Hirschfeld founded the first organization in the defense of homosexuality, the Scientific Humanitarian Committee, and in Berlin in 1874 Adolf Brand founded *Der Eigene, The Special One,* the first magazine to celebrate love between men. In Chicago in 1924 the Prussian Henry Gerber created the first homosexual organization in America, the Society of Human Rights, the building declared a National Historic Landmark in 2015.

The Renaissance of homoeroticism took place in Prussia, and from 1800 to 1933 Berlin progressively mutated into the homosexual capital of the world, the seat of Romanticism, the rebirth of Periclean Greece, where the greatest researchers and psychoanalysts united to justify male-male love, where scientific institutes saw the light of day, supported by even the police who encouraged research into the reasons for the explosion of homosexual clubs, bars and hundreds of boy brothels. Students sought truth and the betterment of society through discussions taking place during hikes and encampments around fires, the participants underscoring their quest for freedom through male bonding and total nudism. Literature, poetry and naked boys filled magazines pinned open at kiosks to reveal the extraordinary beauty of the unclothed body. The last half of this book will be devoted to this liberating phenomenon.

Thomas Mann wrote: ''I have lived and loved. I knew happiness, held in my arms he I longed for.'' To my mind this is the very aim of life. The *only* aim of life. It is the soul of this book, the story of men who preferred men.

The period of Enlightenment and Romanticism (explained later on) coalesced to produce a hundred-year span of friendships between men, friendships among those who shared similar interests and values. These male-male relationships could develop into a sexually neuter friendship in which a man would willingly die for his mate, as found in Australia, or it could develop into something more intimate, where one shared all with his friend, where mutual tears could be shed, kisses exchanged, common interests and common needs coalescing into something passionate and something sensual. Freud's assertion that we are all bisexual at the origin needed little more, at times, to tip the scales from friendship-love to friendship-lust. Greece was never far away, at first Plato-platonic, then Eros-erotic.

I'm a boy of my times, one who prefers vocable like cock to weenie, fuck to liaison. This will be crude and offensive to some readers, but one has to be true to oneself, and today's liberties are to be cherished, even if those liberties have strict limits: a boy today would need undaunted courage to admit to his locker-room buddies that he prefers them to the chirping maidens in the showers next door.

For purists: I use numerals when I think a number is important-- especially age milestones--because they stand out more clearly, no matter how big or small the number. And please forgive my personal interventions during the telling of the lives of these extraordinary men; I try to keep them to a minimum even if, exceptionally, I do intervene more than usual in this book.

And please excuse the lamentable condition of some of the photos, better, I feel, than no photos at all.

PART I

FREDERICK THE GREAT – AN OVERVIEW

Napoleon felt that Frederick was the greatest tactical genius of all time, the reason for his proclaiming, standing above Frederick's grave, ''Gentlemen, if this man were still alive I would not be here.'' Frederick said that the key to his success was foresight, the ability to see the evolution of events in advance. This was followed by the audacity of the attack, destroying the enemy from an unexpected direction, all of which implied, as he further said himself, donning the skins of a lion and a fox. The Seven Years' War made the Prussian reputation as the world's greatest fighting power, one it has to this very day. It was the reason why General Washington bent over backwards to assure himself of the services of von Steuben, the Prussian who had not only been taught by Frederick, but had been Frederick's aide-de-camp. In the Battle of Rossbach Frederick defeated a combined force of French and Austrian troops, 41,000 men, with his own army of 21,000, leaving the field strewn with 10,000 dead to his losses of 550. At the Battle of Leuthen he confronted 80,000 Austrians with his army of 36,000, killing 7,000 and taking 20,000 prisoners. With every battle he risked everything, his army, his kingdom and his life, and he very nearly lost it all more than once. He maintained that wars had to be short if one didn't want the population of be decimated, resources depleted and army discipline weakened.

Frederick and the artist who painted him, Anton Graff

The history of the Polish people that, alas, we won't go into in any detail here, has been sad since its creation, famine, disease, wars, the Poles looked down on by other nations, a country Catherine the Great put her former lover Poniatowski in charge of, in order to rid herself of him and to have a complacent presence in the huge entity that bordered Russia. Frederick himself hated the Poles, calling them ''slovenly trash'', and even today their willingness to work for low wages makes them pariahs who compete with the laborers in other countries throughout Europe. Frederick's interest in Poland was the fact that it stood between two huge segments of Prussia, western Prussia and eastern Prussia, and Frederick wanted both segments united. The Protestant Prussians locked in Catholic Poland wanted freedom of religion, and Frederick, who couldn't have cared less for the religious aspect of things, used their plight as a wedge to free 200,000 Prussian Protestants awash in 11 million Catholic Poles, as Hitler would later do in the Sudetenland.

The idea of partitioning Poland apparently came from Frederick's brother Prince Henry, a boy known for his intelligence, energy and ambition, as well as his insatiable lust for lads. What took place was one of three warless divisions of Poland with Prussia gaining the lands between the two main entities of Prussia, Austria gaining a bigger part still, and Catherine's Russia the lion's share in what is known as the First Partition of Poland in 1772. In addition to joining western Prussia to eastern Prussia, Frederick rebuilt Polish villages, drained marshes, abolished serfdom and sent in Jesuits (despite his being a Protestant) to open schools for the Poles he now called ''vile apes.'' The schools were so successful that he welcomed the Jesuits throughout his own Prussia. He immensely increased trade, bringing Poland economic stability for the first time, and ordered his officials to learn Polish. Grain was distributed throughout the country so that crops could be sown and the population fed, another first for this country the victim of famines; in fact, Poland became a grain exporter. He reformed Polish bureaucracy, encouraged religious tolerance and introduced Prussian justice, renowned for being the best--fastest and most honorable--in Europe. Jews were prompted to establish themselves throughout Frederick's kingdom because they were inimitable traders, bankers and merchants, a vital source of wealth for Prussia. French Huguenots were welcome even more, for possessing the same assets as the Jews and the right religion--Protestantism.

As for Prince Henry, son of Frederick William I, younger brother of Frederick the Great, he was found far superior to Frederick by Voltaire who knew him intimately and thought the lad was a far better strategist than his brother, possessing a better mind, better judgment, whom Voltaire called a veritable man of the Enlightenment, the incarnation of the Philosopher King. One of 13 children, after his father's death Frederick placed him, at age 14, colonel of a regiment. The boy took part in the Battle for Silesia and during the Seven Years' War. Each time Frederick failed to take Henry's counsel he lost or nearly lost battles, and once came within a hair of losing his life. Henry loved boys, and was forced to marry, as did many of his contemporaries for show, perhaps not even once honoring his wife as Frederick had said he had been obliged to do his. Von Steuben, whose life will be fully treated later on, was one of his countless lovers, and even suggested to Alexander Hamilton that America be doted with a king, and that that king be Prince Henry (Steuben, Henry and Hamilton formed a homosexual triumvirate). As the kings of Poland were elected, Henry strove for that position, only to be opposed by his brother. He did, however, work behind the scenes in favor of the First Partition of Poland. The names of three of his lovers have come down to us, the actor Blainville, Count La Roche-Aymon, 17, and his preferred, Major von Kaphengst whom Henry gave a castle and estates, where the major led a fully dissolute, fully gratifying life. Henry ended his days advising Frederick's successor, his nephew Frederick William II, followed by Frederick William III.

The particularity of Prussian rule over eastern Prussia, called the Duchy of Prussia, was that the area would revert to Poland if the Prussians in western Prussia, called Brandenburg, did not produce a male heir, the reason why Prussian kings were kings *in* Prussia and not kings *of* Prussia, until Frederick the Great finally united both segments.

In Berlin he built buildings still in existence, the opera, the Royal Library, St. Hedwig's Cathedral and Prince Henry's Palace, the site of today's Humboldt University. In Potsdam he erected his Sans Souci Palace.

Sans Souci today.

Although German was used when dealing with his army, his preferred language was by far French, and the person he preferred speaking it with was the symbol of the Enlightenment itself, Voltaire. Frederick is said to have spoken English, Portuguese and Spanish, and to have understood Hebrew, Latin and Greek. He felt that German culture had been retarded by wars, especially the Thirty Years' War, as well as those against the Turks and the French. French courts revolted him by their luxury and lack of virility, preferring his own court, infinitely smaller and based on intimate friendships. He was in no way xenophobic and invited inhabitants from other countries to people Prussia, giving them land and encouraging the cultivation of various plants like potatoes, following this up with new canals for irrigation and for use in commerce.

Hunting for him was pursued by the intellectually weak, and his love of horses and dogs was so boundless that he requested being interred with his greyhounds in his simple tomb. He died in his armchair, at 74, but his grave was opened by Hitler who wanted the coffin preserved from bombardments in a salt mine. It was later returned to Sans Souci ''without pomp and at night'' as he had wished, where passersby can stop and reflect on this truly original man.

PRUSSIA – THE SETTING
FREDERICK I

As I wrote in the Introduction, Germany could far more justifiably be called Prussia because Prussia has been the heart, mind and military power behind the German nation since it conception. But the very core of that embryonic conception was Brandenburg, with its capital Berlin.

Brandenburg was one of the seven electorates that voted to elect the Emperor of the Holy Roman Empire, and in 1417 Frederick Hohenzollern, a rich merchant, bought it, becoming, for a sack of gold, Frederick I. Brandenburg was a melting pot of nationalities, many Slaves but also French, Dutch, Italians and others, the working language for whom was Germany, the language of the court French. All were presided over by the Holy Roman Emperor, seated in Vienna, but it was Frederick I who ruled the daily life in Brandenburg. Theoretically anyone could become Holy Roman Emperor. Henry VIII tried, as did François I, but historically the place went to the wealthiest family of the times, male Habsburgs, and as everyone wanted to marry into their family, through dowries and inherited estates they became ever wealthier, ever more powerful.

There then followed the wars of religion and around 1530 the new Brandenburg emperor Joachim II was converted by his mother to Lutheran Protestantism, but because the Holy Roman Emperor Charles V was Catholic, the Hohenzollerns were obliged to be tolerant of other faiths, a tolerance that would characterized Prussians throughout their existence.

Thanks to supremely intelligent marriages, the Hohenzollerns greatly increased their territory, one huge section being the Duchy of Prussia, in Poland, east of Danzig. The result was a kingdom as dispersed as the island of the Pacific, awaiting the genius of Frederick the Great to unit them into one continuous empire.

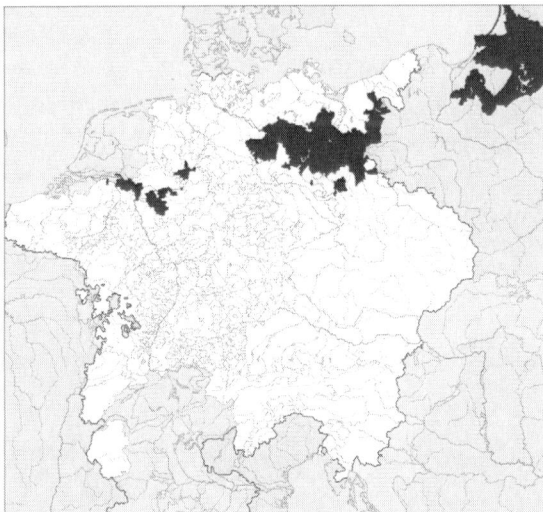

Brandenburg, the dark shade in the upper middle,

FREDERICK WILLIAM (1620 – 1688)

The religious wars were especially hard on Hohenzollern Brandenburg, with armies crisscrossing flat unprotected lands, villages sacked, leaving men hanging from spits where they had been roasted like pigs until screaming out the places where they had hidden their money; naked girls, dead, their legs stretched apart, puddles of blood and semen mingling on the rain drenched ground; children hanged, babies dashed against trees and walls; the whole followed by diseases: typhus, plague and dysentery to name a few. All because men fought over the primacy of this god or that, this tendency or another--Catholic, Lutheran or Calvinist.

Forty years later, just forty, Hohenzollern Brandenburg would have a standing army of 30,000, so powerful their reputation would supersede even that of the Alexander the Great, all due to one man, Frederick William, the spiritual father of Frederic the Great. And Destiny, in its wisdom, desired that he reign 48 years, longer than any Hohenzollern. Raised in the Dutch Republic where his parents had sent him out of harm's way, the Calvinism of the Dutch that his family had then chosen over Lutheranism was reinforced. He learned Polish because of his future ascension over the Duchy of Prussia, as well as French, Dutch and German. Like Peter the Great who had been so enamored of the Dutch that he adopted their flag for Russia, Frederick William too based much of his reign on Dutch/Calvinist rigor in finance and morals, and used the excellent Dutch Army as a model for the Prussian forces soon to become famous. Thanks to his isolation in the Netherlands, he became a ruler who would enhance every aspect of life in his territories, increasing agriculture, building routes and still more canals, and, more even than his ministers, he worked the longest hours and sat the longest time in his councils, a model monarch.

Frederick William

As he was surrounded on all sides by forces that threatened to swallow up Brandenburg and his other lands, Frederick William knew his salvation would come exclusively through the forces he could muster and train, and it was with this in mind that he began a forced march to military self-sufficiency, ending up, as stated, with 30,000 men. For help he drew on what was best in the Swedish, Dutch and French armies, he opened a school for cadets, he fed, dressed and provided good care for his men, including their retirement, and he treated them humanely, the only army where the soldiers were men and not beasts to be beaten into compliance. The cadets were taught French, history, geography, engineering, fencing and dancing, many if not most of them would wind up dead on the battlefield because it was they, most often the sons of the nobility, who led their men, they who were at the forefront of cavalry charges, another Prussian innovation.

The demon after the Thirty Years' War was Charles X of Sweden who planned to expand his empire to the walls of Rome. Charles did invade Frederick William's lands with 14,000 men that Frederick William, apoplectic with fury, met with 8,000 that the Swedes had no idea were coming. Taken by surprise, Frederick William ordered them massacred. A second battle followed, with 11,000 Swedes against 7,000 Brandenburgers who won the day, aided by peasants who refused immense sums of money offered by their captives, for the simple pleasure of slitting the Swedes' throats until their heads fell away from their bodies.

Calvinists were put in top bureaucratic positions, less for religious reasons than their steadfastness, and foreigners were welcome, despite the complaints of Branderburgers who wanted the jobs themselves.

The Thirty Years' War was a major cataclysm that impoverished the nations taking part, brought death to thousands of soldiers and mercenaries, and ended the lives of countless others, farmers whose crops fed the troops and whose girls eased the loins of the invaders, towns sacked and burned because that was a mercenary's only pay, and suffering for all concerned through plagues, diseases and disgusting dysentery; a religious war between Catholics and Protestants, the Holy Roman Empire seeking to stamp out heretics, aided by Spain that wished to crush the Protestant Dutch over whom Spain reigned. Protestant Sweden rose up, establishing itself as a new continental power, and Catholic France joined the Protestants in order to curtail the ascendancy of the Holy Roman Empire.

Frederick William was succeeded by Frederick I (father of Frederick William I, himself father of Frederic (II) the Great). Frederick I was friendly, affable, generous and universally liked, while his son would be brutal, violent, vulgar and a physical danger to his son.

FREDERICK WILLIAM I (1688 – 1740)

Frederick William I took the throne in 1713 and immediately fired 2/3rds of the servants, obliging the rest to take a cut in salary of 75%. He sold the family jewels, gold and silver plate, furniture and coaches, the royal menagerie of lions and whatever else was needed to save his kingdom from bankruptcy, as Frederick I had been profligate to unimaginable extent. A strange equality was set up where Frederick William's advisors, officials and officers conversed with the king on any and all subjects, informal to the point that no one stood for him. They met in a room, men only, amidst drink and tobacco, where the conversation ran from rumors to gossip to newspaper reports and hunting exploits, as well as the sexual adventures of the participants, disclosed in the filthiest terms--and it is said that few languages can be dirtier than German and Latin (thanks to the earthy ancient Romans). Refined practical jokes were played, like surreptitiously giving a man a laxative and then locking him in his room.

Yet Frederick William was an admirable administrator, tireless and conscientious, the proof being the instant economic stability he brought to his court the very moment he crowned himself king. Taxation became so detailed that a farmer was taxed according to the fertility of the soil! Marshes were drained so that more land could produce more food for the people, producing, at the same time, more taxes in support of the government.

Frederick William changed the face of army recruitment. Boys were obliged to put themselves on a list and were called up when there was not enough voluntary enlistment. They received basic training and were then free to return to their old jobs, obliged only to attend courses two months a year until retirement. Peasants and certain trades were exempt (the priority being the production of food and the growth of commerce), as were government employees (needed to govern). Frederick William had parade grounds built outside his office so he could watch drills during the day, drills that became the solid foundation of the Prussian Army, and would later be the foundation of the American Army thanks to the homosexual Prussian von Steuben who would train American troops under General Washington (fully reported later). Soon Frederick William had 80,000 men under his orders. The nobility was obliged to furnish a list of their boys, 12 to 18, from which handsome healthy boys were chosen for his cadet school, to the nobles' fruitless objection. Frederick William had a troop of ''tall lads'', all over 6', and short boys were rarely called up for service. The boys were obliged to wear their uniforms in church, and drilling took place on town grounds, all of which built up, little by little, a sense of worth, and soon being a soldier became an honor.

PART II

FREDERICK THE GREAT (1712 – 1786)

FATHER AND SON

We now arrive at the life of the most important man in Prussian history, and a true world figure known as Frederick the Great. Civil wars are horrors, at times pitting fathers against sons, and what happened between Frederick William and his son Frederick could easily have ended in Frederick William's murdering his boy in one of the rages that characterized him, just as Ivan the Terrible had cut the throat of his son when mad with anger. Frederick William once beat the boy so severely that he told him if his own father had gone so far he would have killed himself in shame, while Frederick took the trouncing like a lowly serf. Such disrespect from a father was endlessly fueled by Frederick himself trying to be too clever, outwardly showing respect while in reality scoffing at Frederick William who knew exactly what the boy was up to. Frederick William, despite his boorish vulgarity, had worked himself to the bone to make Prussia into a veritable powerhouse that he naturally wanted continued by his son. Yet Frederick showed no sign of sharing any of his father's qualities. He was messy, unkempt, he preferred poetry, books and the company of his mother and sister to his father's banquets between men only, and he couldn't even ride a horse without falling off. A boy his father couldn't figure out, and once admitted he would give anything to be able to open his skull to see what was going on in the lad's brain.

The mystery is how Frederick turned out to be one of the world's greatest strategists, going infinitely farther than his father, even if, as we shall see, luck often played an uncannily important part in his successes.

We'll go into the sexual aspect of Frederick's life in the chapter on Algarotti, but for the moment suffice it to say that Frederick wished to marry into English royalty (which had nothing to do with sex and everything to do with ascendancy), a double marriage during which he would be given the hand of Princess Amalia of England and his sister that of the Prince of Wales. But the Holy Roman Emperor, fearing that this would give Prussia too much power, convinced Frederick William to look elsewhere for suitable aspirants. Frederick decided to flee to England accompanied by his lover Hans Hermann von Katte. Both were rounded up, along with other officers, and imprisoned. Frederick was given a questionnaire by his father, the key question asking him if he deserved to be king after dishonoring himself by deserting his regiment, and if not would he therefore renounce his right to the throne in order that his life be spared? Frederick answered that the king would decide if he were to live or die, but although his life did not mean all that much to him, the king would certainly not be so merciless.

Historians nearly unanimously believe that Frederick William was more than capable of putting his son to death, and while waiting to decide he ordered that Frederick be obliged to watch the execution of von Katte, whose head was severed from his body. Von Katte had written to his father, begging him to forgive him for the sorrow he would cause, forgive him for dashing all the hopes his father had had for him, aware that he would not be a comfort in his father's old age, sad that he would die in the spring of his youth, without fulfilling the future his father had so carefully planned for him. Katte also wrote to Frederick William promising to be the most loyal of his officers and begging for clemency, receiving no response. One wonders if Frederick William knew about the love between Katte and his son. As for the others caught up in the tragedy, they were jailed until Frederick became king and freed them all.

von Katte

Of course, we can never know the inner working of the mind, the reasons for our motivations, the reality that one can grow up a choir boy and mute into a butcher of men. We would like to make Shakespearean windows into one's soul, as Frederick William wished in order to understand the workings of his son Frederick. So following the shock of seeing his lover's decapitation Frederick's reaction was so strange, and the reasons for it so lost in the convolutions of his brain, that the truth will never be known. Had he not become great the story would end here. We would not go on to relate how he fell to his knees before the tyrant who had sired him, kissing the boots of the monster who had taken the young life of his lover. But he did become great, and so the story will continue, one perplexing to the writer and the reader, especially when we learn from Nancy Mitford's book *Frederick the Great* that shortly following Katte's martyrdom Frederick was gaily passing the night with new intimates. After his death 30 volumes of his writing would be published, but even then we known nearly nothing about his personal life, less even than we known about some of the key ancient Greeks and Romans who lived thousands of years earlier.

Yet he did fall to his knees, pleading for forgiveness and promising allegiance, and Frederick William, a man suspicious of all and of everything, came to believe his son's repentance and conversion into a mirror image of the father himself. Real or chameleon-like, Frederick became a model student, applying himself to the mastery of affairs, taking over a troop of boys his father accorded him, tirelessly drilling and exercising them, a troop soon to be enlarged to an army when Frederick William accorded more responsibility. Freed from prison, he was allowed to take part in the administration of the town where he was held captive, Küstren, where he learned the fundamentals of bureaucracy. He was even given a wife, a woman who would adore him until her last breath, like a dog boundlessly in love with the master that kicked it way, love as mindless as that which Frederick outwardly showered on his father. Frederick later said he had ''honored'' her, French--his preferred language--for fucking (as there was certainly no *love* involved), and it may have been so, at least *once*. From then on he found satisfaction with men as brilliant as Algarotti (whose story we will cover in full) or as simple as his boy aides-de-camp, but here the mystery is so complete that we run the spectrum of those who believe he had a new recruit every night, to those who maintain that he had somehow been injured when mercury was injected into his genitals as a way of curing syphilis, so mutilated that he could never function sexually again. One of his closest, most intimate friends was Voltaire, *the* personification of the Enlightenment, whom some believe was intimate with Frederick, but who, after falling out with the king, wrote a book listing Frederick's loves, proof that he was in no way impotent--if what Voltaire wrote was true. Voltaire had many homosexual friends, among them Frederick's lover Algarotti, and although Voltaire never hid the fact of his promiscuity, people were nonetheless shocked when they learned that the niece he adored, that he had watched over in her crib, not only lost her virginity to the wizened old man but later followed him from town to town begging for more.

Of course, the inconceivable trauma of seeing his lover decapitated, and the near certainty of his own imminent death, may have changed Frederick, or, as Christopher Clark in his wonderful *Iron Kingdom* (2006) so perfectly put it: ''Did the events of 1730 forge a new artificial persona ... locked within the nautilus hull of a convoluted nature? Or did they merely deepen and confirm a tendency towards self-concealment and dissimulation that was already well developed in the adolescent prince? The question is ultimately unanswerable.''

But, revealingly, after the death of his father Frederick continued on in his father's way. The council of advisors and friends Frederick William had amassed became, if possible, even more masculine, where homoerotic banter flourished, and despite the fact that we ignore what went on in private, we do know that sex and boys were constantly on his mind. Frederick, ever faithful to his life-long need for knowledge, kept up the reading that had begun years before, thanks to his Huguenot teacher Jacques Egide Dunhan de Jandun, who surreptitiously bought him a library of 3,000 volumes, largely Greek and Roman masters. He surrounded himself with the greatest philosophers of the times whom he pleaded to join him at his all-male den Sans Souci, where all his friends remained by his side, says Christopher Clark, until ''they died or betrayed him by taking wives''.

FREDERICK THE GREAT – SILESIA
1740

A high point of Frederick's military career was the taking of Silesia in 1740. Silesia was on the border of Brandenburg and was surrounded by Saxony that Frederick knew wanted to invade Silesia because it was an extremely rich and industrialized part of the Holy Roman Empire. Possessing Silesia would close the gap between the two halves of Saxony, thusly forming a country of huge importance, a scheme that would later inspire Frederick to close up the gap between Brandenburg and the Duchy of Prussia, at Poland's expense. The moment was perfect for Saxony as the English were too weak from their wars with Spain to stop it, Russia was paralyzed by the death of Tsarina Anna, and the Holy Roman Emperor had just died, leaving only daughters to claim a title historically meant to be filled by sons. These were the same reasons Frederick decided on a lightening attack. Days after the death of the Holy Roman Emperor Charles V, Frederick invaded, setting off a European-wide war because other nations and surrounding countries decided, hyena-like, to step in and take their part of the Holy Roman carcass, a conflagration that became known as the War of the Austrian Succession. Frederick, not wanting the total destruction of Austria, signed the Peace of Breslau (1742) with the Holy Roman Empire, bringing peace and the succession of Silesia to Brandenburg.

Silesia circled.

This happy end was naturally too quick and good to be true. After two years of peace, Austria tried to take back Silesia, ending in another victory for Frederick with the Peace of Dresden in 1745, the whole finalized in the Peace of Aix-la-Chapelle, signed in 1748 by Britain and France that guaranteed Prussian possession of Silesia, although, significantly, Austria did not sign. Austria did sign a treaty with Russia, a secret clause of which called for the invasion of Hohenzollern lands, meaning basically Brandenburg and the Duchy of Prussia, with Austria regaining Silesia.

Marie Theresa, the daughter of Charles V and the new empress of the Holy Roman Empire, had signed the Peace of Aix-la-Chapelle in order to give her time to raise a bigger, stronger army and form more powerful alliances, which this absolutely extraordinary woman did, a worthy descendant of Eleanor d'Aquitaine and Catherine de' Medici. She eventually organized her army along Prussian lines and, just as important, she cared for her troops who in turn fought to the death for her.

The victory of a small state, Prussia, against an entire Empire was enormous but not entirely complete in that it brought to light two symbols that were to characterize Frederick's rule: reckless audacity and dumb good luck. That he invaded so rapidly has all historians admiringly saluting his audacity, while labeling it foolhardy. And during one battle, that of Mollwitz, he was so certain he had been defeated that he fled the field, although Prussian training--and luck--brought the Prussians, in the end, victory, even if the victory had been terribly costly in human lives lost. But bit-by-bit he gained in confidence and strategic planning.

FREDERICK THE GREAT - THE SEVEN YEARS' WAR
1756 – 1763

When war between Britain and France broke out in 1754 Frederic saw his chance at both expansion and to strike against Saxony, an aggressive threat on his borders, by simply seizing the country.

Saxony circled, seized by Frederick in 1756.

This set off a chain reaction of alliances: Austria joined forces with France in hopes of regaining Silesia, Britain joined forces with Prussia against France, and Russia aligned with Austria against Prussian expansion until one of history's greatest and most unexpected *coups de théâtre* took place--another proof of Frederick's incredible luck: Tsar Peter III came to the throne and joined forces with Frederick whom the Russian boy-king worshipped.

During the war Frederick won some battles so impressively that it's extremely hazardous to guess how he did it: at the Battle of Rossbach for example his 20,000 Prussians came up against 40,000 French, and when the firing ended 10,000 French bodies were strewn over the battlefield to 500 Prussian losses.

On the other hand the new Holy Roman Empress, Maria Theresa, had had her troops trained in Prussian tactics, so when Frederick tried his signatory oblique attack the Austrians were ready, leaving 14,000 dead Prussians to nurture the sol of Kolin, against 8,000 Austrian lads.

Frederick won against Russia during the Battle of Zorndorf, but lost 13,000 men to Russia's 18,000. That Russia, by far Frederick's most deadly foe, then withdrew, thanks to Peter, was a colossal miracle. Then Catherine the Great had her husband Peter III murdered, but she did not reenter the conflict--still more dumb luck for Frederick. That said, no other army at the time was as cruel as the Russians, for whom simply maiming was not an alternative to cutting off noses and ears before disemboweling men, women and children, and neither sex--men nor women--had to necessarily be alive to undergo the bestiality of sexual assaults. By the end of the Seven Years' War 400,000 Prussians had lost their lives.

FREDERICK THE GREAT – THE PARTITIONS OF POLAND

1772

The disappearance of Poland in 1795, a country bigger than France, is the most incredible incongruity in history. A first partition took place between Frederick's Prussia and Catherine's Russia in 1772. For Frederick the act of joining western Prussia to eastern Prussia, creating the all-powerful entity seen in the map below, was the immense triumph of his reign. Long before the reality of the partition he had recognized Poland as being the sick man of Europe, and compared the country to an artichoke that he would devour one leaf at a time. Poland had an elected monarchy that anyone from any nation could hold: the supremely homosexual Henry III (5) became its monarch thanks to the tireless efforts and monies of his mother, the inimitable Catherine de' Medici, and Catherine the Great herself had placed her lover Poniatowsky on the country's throne as a way of directing its every move and of freeing her bedroom for the young soldiers she spotted from the windows of her palace, healthy males whose warmth she herself claimed she needed every single day.

The result of an elective monarchy and a vague constitution led to anarchy outside of Poland's borders (anarchy between states that quarreled over who would possesses her) and civil disturbances within, anarchy the invaders used as an excuse for ''saving'' the country by biting off chunks of it, the largest for Russia, 13%, the next largest for Austria, 12%, and what was needed by Frederick to unite Brandenburg to the Duchy of Prussia, 5%.

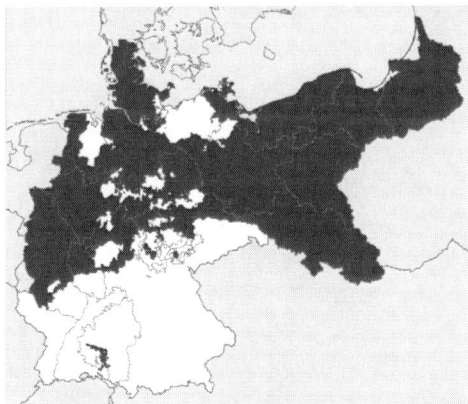

Kingdom of Prussia at its greatest.

Frederick had a unique and quasi-absolute respect for freedom of expression, allowing it in the press and even permitting the circulation of

Voltaire's book entailing his homosexual encounters. He fought for the rights of the common man, the most sensational case, one that had the citizenry on the edge of their seats, was the trial against a miller, Arnold, who refused to pay his noble landlord rent when said landlord cut off the supply of water to Arnold's mill, diverting it into fish ponds for the noble's own use. Three courts found Arnold guilty, infuriating Frederick to the point that he had the third verdict's judges jailed for a year. The next trial found Arnold innocent and he was reimbursed for the totality of his losses.

FREDERICK THE GREAT – ALGAROTTI
1712 - 1764

In another intercession into the justice of his country, Frederick personally intervened in the case of a peasant who had penetrated his donkey sexually, stating that a man had the right to put his penis wherever he wished. He welcomed Julien Offray de la Mettrie to his court, the author of the *Art of Orgasm* and the *Little Guy with the Big Cock*. Baculard d'Arnaud, another friend, penned *The Art of Fucking* and Frederick was said to have written erotic prose lost to us. An unknown source published that Frederick fucked stable boys, pages, recruits and whoever else came his way during the day. Voltaire who knew his intimate side better than any source outside Frederick's court wrote that Frederick enjoyed a boy as soon as he rose in the morning, a lackey or a cadet, adding that it was Frederick the bottom.

La Mettrie's unbridled sexuality was expressed in his book *Discours sur le bonheur*, an appeal to hedonistic pleasure that was said to have shocked Voltaire and Diderot, men *pourtant* known for their unbridled libertinage. La Mettrie was a doctor, and in addition to his no-holds-barred erotic palaver with Frederick he was used as a court physician. He is said to have died of indigestion following a meal in which he downed a platter of *pâté de faisan aux truffes*.

Frederick's most famous entanglement was with Algarotti, an Italian, one of the Italian boys who have fulfilled the desires of Germans and Brits since well before Byron made Italian lads his personal reserve.

The story of Algarotti will bring the life of Frederick full circle, and in order to tell it fully I'm going to allow myself great leeway in the repetition of some aspects of Frederick's life already covered, the aim of which is full discloser and a story with no loose ends.

Francesco Algarotti must have been wondrously beautiful because the path he trod was lined with loving hearts, some broken perhaps, but Algarotti did what he could to make one and all happy, and this to the end of his life.

Algarotti later in life.

One drawn-out affaire consisted of an English couple, a man, John Hervey, and Hervey's sometime mistress, Mary Montagu, a bisexual threesome of Feydeauesque dimensions. Both strove to win Algarotti's love, both succeeded for a while. Hervey was wise enough to not rope the boy in, and to not bore him with zealous pleas for his presence; Montagu's pleading was incessant, and she left family, husband and children to take up residence in Italy, in hopes of intercepting Algarotti during one of his passages there. As in Feydeau, one left the boy's presence through one door, while a second door immediately opened and a famished suitor entered, throwing himself/herself to Algarotti's feet.

Hervey

At the time Mary Montagu was over the hill, Hervey was 40, ''a ridiculous figure, powdered and rouged, with not a tooth in his head'' ... although he possessed ''the best set of Egyptian pebbles (false teeth) you ever saw,'' wrote the Duchess of Marlborough to a friend. Algarotti was 24, ''dazzlingly good-looking, with wavy raven hair swept back from is brow and coal-black eyes,'' says Lucy Moore in her book on Hervey, *Amphibious Thing, The Life of a Georgian Rake*, a much needed work on the man. Moore tells us something about the sexuality of the times: A certain Mathieu Marais describes a scene taking place in a palace where the young Duc de Bouffiers tried to sodomize the willing Marquis de Rambure. When

Bouffiers didn't succeed his brother-in-law, the Marquis d'Alincourt, stepped in and finished the job for him. This in a public room in front of witnesses.

But beauty was one thing, intelligence another, and in Algarotti's case both appear limitless. He was admitted to the Royal Society as a member, a distinguished honor won through real and solid expertise. Algarotti had his in optics, penning his famous *Newtonism for Ladies* in 1737, just the title of which is an invitation to enter into the world of fun and games at Algarotti's side. He wrote a thesis on language, another on the opera, one on architecture, another on Horace and on painting.

Born in Venice to wealthy parents, his education was deep and complete, his interests as varied as those of a true Renaissance Man-- although he was born during the Enlightenment--patterned on his predecessor the humanist Cosimo de' Medici.

Elegant and sophisticated, his love affaires were ceaseless, taking him, in the company of the rich, famous and intelligent, through Florence, Rome, Paris, Vienna, Turin and Prussia, to name but a few watering holes, finding time to take the baths with Voltaire in Kleve, who called the boy his swan. Frederick was certainly not the great love of Algarotti's life but Frederick was by far the most influential. Frederick was said to have adored the boy, which was a comeback of sorts from an adolescence of terror and horror: Young Frederick had been ardently in love with one of his father's pages, 13-year-old Peter Karl Christoph Keith who kept him informed of the king's every action. The king, Frederick William, was a martinet who regulated his son's every movement and was known to strike men on the face with his cane, hardly daring for a person backed by an army. A religious fanatic, he justified his deeds as being in the service of *Gott*, even when he kicked a woman in public. He mercilessly beat his son too, also in public. He wanted him suffocated in religious nonsense, but the boy, aided by his teacher Jacques Duhan, procured a library of 3,000 Greek and Roman classics, as well as books on philosophy and other matters, a personal Renaissance which allowed Frederick to escape his father's religious fanaticism. He did become a pragmatic Calvinist, which meant earning one's way through hard work. How much of a believer he was is unknown, but his faith was minimal.

Peter was replaced by another lad, a deeper love that saw both boys through early years of military service. The lad, become a man, was Hans Hermann von Katte. Both plotted to escape to freer havens, in this case England, but were betrayed by his young lover Peter's brother, for unknown motives. Both Frederick and Katte, plus other army friends, were captured and imprisoned and all, including Frederick, were threatened with death for treason, as they were army officers. The king might well have carried out the execution of his son, as the fanatic Ivan the Terrible did two hundred years before, knifing his boy in the neck, as Abraham was ordered by his god to slit his boy Isaac's throat. Frederick was stripped of his rank and sent to Küstrin for more military indoctrination. He was also forced to marry and wrote to his beloved sister that he was contemplating suicide. He may never have bedded his wife, and after his father's death he visited her once a year in her own palace. She was nonetheless said to have been devoted to him until the end of her life.

Hans Hermann von Katte and his mausoleum.

Frederick was a friend of Voltaire's, a friendship that lasted all of both their lives, with ups-and-downs to the extent that during one of their cooler periods Voltaire wrote and published his *The Private Life of the King of Prussia,* outing Frederick sexually and listing his numerous male lovers. Frederick never commented on it, and later their friendship resumed. The leading intellectual of the Enlightenment, Voltaire was a poet, a philosopher, a playwright, a *touche-à-tout*. He defended homosexuals and he certainly knew a plethora, but nothing indicates he ever touched a boy, other than a friendly French accolade. He once said of Frederick, ''He's a likeable whore.''

Frederick's physician Johann Georg Ritter von Zimmermann claimed that Frederick's privates had been severely damaged during an operation to save his life from a severe form of venereal disease, which may have made him sexually inoperative, but this is pure speculation.

Frederick's grave marker.

Algarotti seems to have left Hervey by the wayside, which we shall do also, after a few words concerning his destiny. Hervey had become sexually active thanks to boarding-school pleasures, the passive prey of boys who appreciated his effeminacy. He was nonetheless described as also being heterosexually active, bedding laundresses and other women who came within his reach. He received a Masters of Arts from Cambridge and wrote poetry, ''as did everyone of that period,'' claimed his mistress and aforementioned rival for Algarotti's favors, Mary Montagu.

He was called Sporus by fellow students, after Nero's bride whom he had had castrated, which reveals volumes about Hervey. He sported an eye patch when in the mood (although it is said that he also did so because one of his eyes constantly watered), powdered his hair and wore white make-up, as did Barry Lyndon in the justly famous film of the same name, as a sexual lure (incomprehensible, perhaps, to modern sensibilities).

He married Mary Lepell who gave him eight children, a woman he visited the time needed to impregnate her, before wandering off with some boy or other, or several at the same time, as was the case in his infatuation with the young Henry Fox before meeting Henry's older brother Stephen, 23, with whom he traveled for fifteen months, the obligatory Grand Tour, to Paris, Rome, Naples and Florence, while his wife pined away between pregnancies. He would occasionally return to her side, accompanied by Stephen whom she adored, and nine months later a baby would be born.

Hervey was known to be physically frail, and Stephen was known to leave his body covered with bruises from his virile passage, all duly noted by Hervey's physician. Active with women, he was most certainly the bottom for men. Accused of such by a member of Parliament, in whose ranks Hervey also served, he challenged his accuser, William Pulteney, to a duel. We must remember that at the time hundreds of men were being burned alive, beheaded, hanged, garroted and drowned like cats (250 in Holland alone, reported during the years 1730-1731) for committing sodomy, an accusation that could not, therefore, be taken lightly. Hervey is said to have fainted after being run through--a mere flesh wound--by Pulteney's sword. He recovered but found himself ridiculed in the press and on stage, and even an opera, *The Intriguing Courtier*, was staged, with him the principle sap.

Stephen was undisputedly the love of Hervey's life. Even when Stephen was 30 Harvey wrote him: ''No business can ever make me neglect what you desire, or prevent my finding time to do anything you say would give you a moment's pleasure.'' During this period they had male lovers, but in their correspondence these adventures, with the exception of Hervey's affaire with the Prince of Wales, were not mentioned. On the other hand, they were proud to vaunt their masculine side by revealing frequent intercourse with girls, causing no jealousy because women were considered inferior to men to such an extent that they could never threaten a male-male relationship, which was on a higher level. As Hervey wrote to Stephen, "I shall always find far inferior pleasure to amuse me in those less grateful hours when you are absent," i.e., helping maidens free themselves from "what they are weary": their virginity.

But time had gone by and the fire had grown lower. Stephen was obliged to remain with his constituency and Hervey complained "How can you prefer making your constituents drunk, to making your friend happy?" Their letters grew fewer and farther between, the subjects less intimate.

Then Stephen decided to marry, the 13-year-old daughter of his brother Henry's mistress, who was 14 years older than Henry, and had introduced Henry to conjugal pleasures when he was but a boy, not forgetting that Hervey had initiated him into the similar pleasures with lads. Stephen's girl was described as "low and childish", and from now on when Stephen came to see Hervey he was accompanied by his young bride and her mother. Naturally, the men could have found a place to be intimate, but there were no longer long and loving afternoons and nights entwined in the same bed. Then Hervey learned that Stephen's wife opened his letters to Stephen, after which he could write nothing of a personal nature. No more assurances of love. No more tidbits of gossip. Their love had run its course. The boy had become a man, the man … old.

He went on to have an affaire with the Prince of Wales, son of King George II, that Hervey himself likened to that of Alexander and Hephaestion. The prince carried a snuffbox with Hervey's portrait, even though the prince was said to have been more a womanizer than even Hervey. In fact, they seemed to have had a falling-out over a certain Anne Vane, that both were enjoying at the same time. Anne had a child that the Prince of Wales' sister attributed to a triumvirate, as Anne had a third lover, Lord Harrington. She soon died, after which the prince and Hervey renewed their friendship. He still met with Stephen, twice weekly for, as he put it, his personal pleasure. He wrote that he liked Stephen's rough sex.

In the meantime Mary Montagu was scouring Italy in search of her beloved Algarotti--Venice, Rome, Genoa, Naples and then Turin where their roads finally crossed. But an unbridgeable rift had developed between them, for reasons not known, other than the simplest fact of life: When it's over, it's over; one can never go back; and one should never try. He went on to Berlin; she to Avignon, a wondrously beautiful town, and died, presumably of boredom.

Hervey broke with Stephen after 15 years of shared warmth and, certainly, moments of sincere love. He died from frail health, before his father, but he left behind three sons.

Stephen's brother Henry, Hervey's lover before Stephen, went on to have a son who became Foreign Secretary.

As for Stephen, he had nine children and his marriage was said to have been happy and fulfilling for both. He became an earl and chose the motto: Don't Tell.

Algarotti filled his world with young lovers to the end, remaining friends with Frederick who filled *his* life by bedding young recruits. When Algarotti died Frederick had a mausoleum raised to him, while reserving a simple stone for himself.

What else is there to say? Both Frederick and Algarotti used life and allowed life to use them, giving and taking like the eternal tides, the very reason for living. The only reason for living.

Algarotti's tomb

PART III

FRIEDRICH WILHELM VON STEUBEN
(1730 – 1794)

Now that we've finished with the life of Frederick II we will discover that of one of his students, who had also been one of Frederick's many aides-de-camp, meaning a lad he had been intimate with. Many historians believe that it was the expertise of Steuben that allowed the army of General Washington to boot their fellow Englishmen from King George's America. Steuben's homoerotic statue stands a few paces from today's Whitehouse, and his gravesite is visited by gays, like lovers in ancient Hellas visited the temple dedicated to Iolaus, the first man to introduce the Greeks to the love of boys (3). This is Steuben's story:

Steuben engaged in homosexual acts in Germany, acts which forced him to flee to Paris in search of employment, acts that set the French clergy against him, forcing him to take the ship *L'Heureux* to America, accompanied by secretaries, translators and an aide-de-camp, all young--

one 17--and all handsome. Perhaps he wished to set up a homosexual court in the country of his adoption, one resembling that of Frederic the Great that he had known intimately, as in America he surrounded himself with loving and handsome boys, two of whom he adopted and left his fortune.

In America the reputation he had concocted for himself, a lieutenant general in Frederic the Great's court, a sophisticated and elegant baron of aristocratic roots (although his was the poorest of the nobility), and despite his swearing like a sailor (or thanks to it), he gained the devotion of those in his service, as well as the troops under his command, and in many cases his men and his boys were said to have even been passionate in their adoration. Yet unlike the youths that flocked to Frederick's palaces due to the king's limitless wealth and power, Steuben in the colonies was in his late forties, bandy-legged and potbellied, as poor as a church mouse, a man who may have drawn many of the youths to his service in the way the historian William Benemann perfectly described his ''angel'', Benjamin Walker: ''Walker had no scruples about exploiting the Baron's sexual interest although he had no intention of reciprocating.'' Unless letters miraculously turn up to prove the contrary, we'll simply never know what his adopted ''sons'' agreed to do in the mystery of the Steuben household, where he paid all the bills and, despite never-ending debt, kept one and all in near opulence through wild borrowing. When Steuben saw Walker the first time he said, ''If I had seen an angel from Heaven I should not have more rejoiced.''

William (Bill/Billy) North was Steuben's gorgeous aide-de-camp in 1779. The historian William Benemann believed North, Walker and Steuben were sexually involved. Both North and Walker received half of Steuben's estate at his death, North turning over his part to his military companions. He retired a brigadier general, enriched by six sons and daughters.

Son of a Royal Prussian Engineer, Friedrich von Steuben was born in 1730. He had the great privilege of accompanying his father to Russia and, at age 14, volunteering with his father in the War of the Austrian Succession (that we learned about in the chapters on Frederick the Great). At age 16 he joined the Royal Prussian Army, was wounded in battle and imprisoned in Russia before becoming a captain and Frederick the Great's aide-de-camp, the traditional position of Frederick's boy lovers, one that dated back to even Richard Coeur de Lion because the boys were present in the tents of the kings as servants and protectors while the kings slept.

In 1762 Frederick himself taught a class in the Art of War with just 13 students, one of which was Steuben. Here he learned advanced strategy and army leadership under the king, a master on the subject. Frederick led his men in common drills, a task disdained by officers in all other armies in the world, but one that made the Prussians the greatest fighting force since the Spartans, as I've already underlined. Steuben's mastery would later take the rabble he found at Valley Forge and change it into the disciplined army that would see the British flee back to England. Prussian officers were taught to care for their men, to see they were warmly dressed, well fed and clean. The Prussians had a particularity: although the men's training was harsh, they were rarely beaten, rarely punished corporally. No army could load a musket faster--eleven seconds--nor march in more perfect formation. French was the language spoken by Frederick the Great and by his court, and no officer could advance through the ranks without it, although German was used with the troops.

Steuben had come to Frederick's notice when, as a prisoner in Russia, he had learned that Tsarina Elizabeth, Frederic's implacable nemesis, had died and had been replaced by Tsar Peter III, for whom Frederick was a living god. This allowed Frederick to sign a peace treaty with Russia, to take Steuben on as his aide, and to introduce Steuben to his brother Prince Henry, a notorious homosexual who appreciated Steuben's good looks and took him into his own quarters as a staff member.

Steuben was discharged from the army in 1763, most probably because an enemy in the army used Steuben's homosexuality as a tool to rid himself of his presence. A letter to an intimate friend at the time, Captain von Lüttwitz, has come down to us: "You know me too well to feel that my friendship for you could ever become lukewarm. My dear Orestes, your Pylades loves you as loyally as he has ever loved you. His friendship to you shows no change. Not the remotest distance can diminish it."

He found work as a court chamberlain to the Prince of Hohenzollern-Hechigen that he held for three years. During this time he received a huge medal, the Order of Fidelity, from a minor German prince, a medal he let people believe came from Frederick the Great himself. He lost his position as chamberlain when his preference for young boys became so frequent that it caused a scandal among those in the know.

Steuben with his huge medal, on the right, a decoration he was never without.

He moved to Paris where he met Benjamin Franklin who was looking for experienced officers to serve in the American Continental Army, if they would do so on a voluntary basis, since the Continental Congress had no funds. Because he was always in dire need of money, Steuben planned to look for employment elsewhere. Alas, although homosexuality posed little problem in Prussia, in the rest of Europe it was not tolerated, especially Steuben's brand of sex that had young boys for his prey. Broke and becoming old, he had little choice other than board the *L'Heureux* to the American colonies with, in his baggage, Pierre-Etienne Duponceau, 17, his interpreter; Carl Vogel, a boy manservant; Jean-Baptiste de Francy, a ''friend''; 20-year-old Augustin François Des Epiniers, Francy's friend; and Louis de Ponthière, Steuben's aide-de-camp. (Pictures of whom cannot be found.)

In America he was greeted by the president of the Continental Congress, Henry Laurens, who appreciated Steuben so much he placed his 23-year-old son, John Laurens, General Washington's pretty aide-de-camp, under Steuben's wing. John ''fell in love with [Steuben] on sight,'' Paul Lockhart tells us in his wonderful book *The Drillmaster of Valley Forge*, as did John Lauren's friend, Alexander Hamilton, a man known for his admiration of beautiful boys. Lockhart says it best: Steuben ''regaled them with tales of bloody battles ... massive cavalry charges at the point of the bayonet, of warrior-kings and glittering courts. He could converse with them on topics ranging from infantry tactics to the works of Seneca,

Cervantes, and Voltaire. He represented a touch of Enlightenment sophistication--something for which the young Laurens and Hamilton were starved--in the rough-hewn society of the camp.'' *Captain* von Steuben, by the way, now introduced himself as a *lieutenant general* under Frederick the Great.

Laurens and Hamilton.

There are some major surprises when one reads of Steuben's American adventure. One is George Washington's incredible attention to detail. He read report after report from Steuben that he fully analyzed and then responded to, even though he was receiving hundreds of documents weekly, from generals, Continental Congress members and other men of immense importance that he was also answering in detail with letters written in his own personal hand, a workload that boggles the imagination, and yet each answer--to enquiries, plans and suggestions on a myriad of subjects, plus ultimatums from prima donna officers like Steuben--was measured and intelligent.

At the same time, Washington knew exactly what was in the minds of the foreigners that advanced their services, the perfect example of which was Steuben himself. Washington wrote that the foreigners at first claimed to be volunteers until the moment they were engaged. Then came their demands to be reimbursed for their travel to America, plus funds to pay for superb clothing, their servants and assistants, horses and a carriage, titles, pensions, land, awards, recognition, especially from Congress, all of which, again, personified Steuben. Yet Washington was such a superior being that despite all this he could judge a man's intrinsic worth and give him what he deserved, as he did with Steuben and Lafayette.

The second surprise was the lamentable condition of Washington's army: the men starving, lacking in clothing to the point that some issued forth in their filthy drawers only. Disease, illness, horrifying weather, abominable cold that destroyed the vibrancy, health and, yes, even the beauty of the youths at Valley Forge and elsewhere in a single season.

A surprise too was the inability of the British to bring the Continentals to heel. They had men, uniforms, food and leaders who were certainly courageous, but they spent their time in settlements, disdaining engagements that would have wiped out the Continental Army, because some Continental Army companies were reduced to one or two men, and others had no officers. America would have eventually become a nation, but how it did so then was a miracle.

Another surprise was the real importance of foreigners in the American war effort. Lafayette was courageous and he led American troops to victories. Of Steuben Lafayette said, "Anyone can teach soldiers how to drill," but although this was a vital segment of Steuben's job, Steuben also taught American soldiers discipline to the extent that even during the loss of a battle, they withdrew *in order*, never stampeding, never throwing away their muskets, as had been the case before and, during the Civil War, would be the case again. Steuben gave the men confidence in themselves because they knew, for the first time, what they were doing, and they did it with exactitude and expertise--exclusively thanks to Steuben. Steuben introduced latrines, a far cry from the men's relieving themselves just outside their tents as had been the case. He ordered cleanliness. He made them care for the clothing he finally forced the Continental Congress to give them to wear. He saw to it that they got better food too, although it at times lacked to the point of near starvation and open mutiny. Steuben was not ashamed to tell the officers that although they could not become friends with the men, that, indeed, there had to be a distance between them, they were nonetheless to love those under them. They were to drill the men themselves, not leaving the job to underlings. Alexander the Great had loved his men too, forging an army that conquered the world--until he made them kowtow to him like some kind of Persian god, at which time they revolted and he lost it all.

Steuben was gruff with the men, he swore at them in German and then got his assistants to repeat the swearing in English, to the immense pleasure of the soldiers. In such touches he made them understand that he cared. That he was homosexual certainly helped but it could just as easily have been a handicap, as in the case of Jack Nicholson during the Indian Mutiny of 1835, a man so disgusted with his own homosexuality that he distanced himself from his soldiers (1).

The final surprise concerning Steuben was his hold over the young men, young Europeans who came over to America with him and young

Americans, in their early twenties and handsome. He was cultivated despite the foul language he favored, he joked, he was amusing, he put one at ease; and he was worldly, certainly more so than the boys surrounding him, even though most of his American assistants came from wealthy backgrounds, had had excellent educations and fathers of intellectual and political prominence.

Lockhart reports a moving story that took place at West Point where Steuben was stationed a short time. Steuben noticed the surname of a boy, Jonathan Arnold, the name of the traitor Benedict Arnold, whose British accomplice, John André, Steuben and others had sentenced to be hanged at the conclusion of a trial Steuben had been a member of. Steuben questioned him as to his relationship to the traitor. The boy said how much he hated carrying the burden and Steuben suggested that he simply take Steuben's own, which the boy did, becoming Jonathan Steuben. Steuben then applied for a lifetime pension for the boy of two dollars per month, which was granted (the precise reason why is, alas, unknown). Both remained lifetime friends.

Around this time Steuben wrote *Regulations for the Order and Discipline of the Troops of the United States*, dubbed the blue book after its color, in French that Duponceau translated into English. In a 2009 auction a first edition sold for $8,540.

Time and again Steuben failed to engage the British, either because the Continental Army wasn't ready, or the Brits were far more numerous, or the necessary orders were not forthcoming due to haggling among Washington's officers, or refusal from the Continental Congress that held the purse strings. In one case he received orders to leave a site, orders that were immediately countermanded, but the soldier carrying them was intercepted by the British, due to which Steuben missed out on another battle. Although he had done his utmost to train the troops and supply them, most were still untrained, underfed and clothed in all but rags. American generals opposed other American generals and they *all* opposed the foreigner dear to Washington's heart, Steuben, who couldn't even speak their language and, worse, was being promoted over their heads. State governors and congressmen further hampered Steuben's efforts to feed and clothe his men by disputing every dime, interested exclusively in their own advancement and wealth. How all of this led to the independence of America is, again, a perplexing enigma, but somehow the Americans got it right, and then somehow they got it right a second time by eventually making Washington the first president, a symbol of America's luck and resilience.

Steuben was brutally frank and direct in his treatment of officers, totally lacking in subtlety, while bending over backwards to be good to his men. In one incident a colonel brought him a recruit, a mere child, that

Steuben, in a rage, sent home while ordering the colonel to take the boy's place in the ranks! His English was still terrible and it was certainly partially the cause of his invectives and foul language, in German, through frustration. In the opera *Billy Budd*, Billy, a stammerer, unable to cry out his outrage at being falsely accused of being a traitor, kills his accuser, through frustration, a man himself shackled by his unrequited love for Billy.

In the meantime France was sending boats and men and muskets, the latter into Steuben's grateful hands. Lafayette was busy at the front, well provided for by his servants, by provisions the officers seemed to have had in abundance, something that could not be said for the soldiers who received nothing of the gold dispatched from France by Louis XVI who would soon, very soon, lose his head to the guillotine. The French admiral de Grasse landed 3,200 French troops while the French controlled the seas off Chesapeake. That the French were so actively providing for the Americans is an additional and welcome surprise in my research, as I am French.

The lack of engagement with the enemy eventually saw Steuben accused of both incompetence and cowardice, and because he didn't lack in enemies his position was fragile. But he had Washington's backing, and after the surrender of the British at Yorktown Washington asked him to train the troops to perfection, as there still remained N.Y. to liberate. An amphibious landing was prepared by Steuben, as well as complicated drills that Washington presented in a demonstration to the French as proof of the Continental Army's professionalism. Steuben also brought the use of bayonets back into play. Each musket had one but they were used by the Americans as they used knives, literally to cut up meat and to spear it from the frying pan. Yet the bayonet was a deadly weapon, and by the time Steuben finished drilling the troops they were adept at its proper function. The result was an immense victory for Steuben and his reputation. Never had the Americans been better prepared for war.

Although the British still possessed N.Y., Washington knew the war was over and, due to the incredible expense, he ordered Steuben to demob, which Steuben wanted to do with a huge parade, one that would show the men that they were the brave heroes of a profoundly grateful nation. But congress refused the funds and so they were left to their own devises, wandering off singly or in small groups, their back pay in the form of promissory notes, and ''a few scraps of food,'' Lockhart tells us, although they could keep their muskets. To one group of men trickling away Steuben was heard lamenting, continues Lockhart, ''March! Into the river and drown yourselves.''

Yet his men would not forget him. To this very day there are Von Steuben Days celebrated by German-Americans in many cities like N.Y.

and Chicago, an American warship and submarine were named for him, as well as an ocean liner. There is a Steuben County in both N.Y. and Indiana, and a Steubenville in Ohio. He has his statue in Lafayette Square near the White House and his home, Steuben House, is a tourist attraction. There is even a Steuben Football Field at Hamilton College, fitting as both he and Alexander Hamilton had been admirers of virile male athletes.

Steuben's homoerotic monument in Lafayette Square and Steuben House.

In retirement at what is known as Steuben House, he sent Congress messages, some asking for money, others proposing that the U.S. set up a standing army, assuring Congress that they had nothing to fear as an army would be made up of their sons and brothers. He also gave details for a military academy, the foundation of the future Annapolis and West Point. He became friends with Washington's vice-president John Adams' son Charles, the homosexual black sheep of the Adams' family, and housed for a time Charles Adams' intimate friend, 19-year-old John Mulligan (to Steuben's age of 62), to whom Steuben left his library and $2,500, an immense sum. Charles later distinguished himself by running naked across the campus of Harvard before succumbing to drink at age 30.

CHARLES ADAMS IN HIS
YOUTH.

As another general put it, age is a shipwreck (de Gaulle: *la vieillesse est un naufrage*). And as I've already gone into his bequests to his boys, North and Walker, both married with families, Walker a Congressman, we can leave this truly remarkable Prussian-American here in peace.

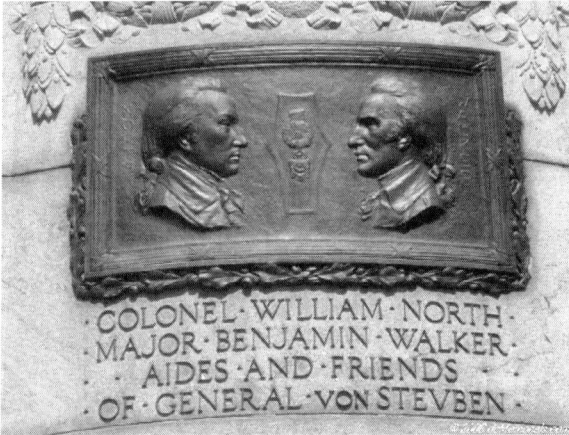

COLONEL·WILLIAM·NORTH·
MAJOR·BENJAMIN·WALKER·
·AIDES·AND·FRIENDS·
·OF·GENERAL·VON·STEVBEN·

Billy North and Benjamin Walker, lovers and Steuben's friends until the end of his life, Steuben lucky up to his last breath.

PART IV

FREDERICK WILLIAM III (1744 – 1840)

The French Revolution was welcomed because the French people's hatred of Louis XVI's wife, the Austrian Marie Antoinette, would mean the severance of ties between France and Austria, Austria being Prussia's most hated enemy. Austria saw the writing on the wall and decided to make peace with Prussia in a treaty that brought support to Louis XVI, both countries recognizing that if he fell, the kings of Austria and Prussia could be endangered by the dissidents in their own domains. France declared war and Austria and Prussia issued a statement saying that neither kingdom wanted territorial expansion in France *if* the French supported their king Louis XVI. Otherwise the revolutionary powers then in charge would face the consequences of their misrule.

During this disorder Catherine the Great decided on a further partition of Poland, which took place in 1793, Prussia inheriting territory that included Danzig, and then a third and last partition in 1795 which saw Russia again taking the lion's share while Prussia got Warsaw, meaning that Poland no longer existed. But where Poland had once been a buffer between Russia and Prussia, Prussia now had Catherine and her Russian troops as its neighbor, Cossack soldiers known for their merciless barbarism.

Everything changed with the coming of Napoleon. France decided that its ''natural boundaries'' extended to the Rhine and immediately sent troops there, with both the Holy Roman Empire and Prussia throwing in the towel by signing whatever treaties they were offered, in the hope of not being cannibalized as they themselves had swallowed up Poland. But the pressure from France was such that in 1806 Austria announced, to the indifference of the world, that the Holy Roman Empire had come to an end, hoping in this way to save the last enclave, Austria itself.

Frederick William III replaced his father in 1797 but his declarations of neutrality didn't stop Napoleon's advance, whose withering cannon fire destroyed the Prussian military--and especially its elite officers who insisted on filling the front ranks. Even so, to his credit, Frederick William III decided to fight on at the side of Russia, despite his ministers who advised him to allow Napoleon to use Prussia as a staging area for an ultimate attack on the Russians. A treaty was nonetheless signed between Napoleon and Tsar Alexander in 1807 as shown in the following picture, a signing ceremony that Frederick William III observed from the bank, having not been invited.

Napoleon and Tsar Alexander signing a treaty of peace on a raft in the middle of the Memel River.

Prussia was reduced in size to Brandenburg, East Prussia (the former Duchy of Prussia) and Silesia. Incredibly, Frederick William sent his wife to beg Napoleon for more land, which was not accorded. Because Saxony had changed sides in Napoleon's favor early on, it was awarded new territory and Napoleon himself crowned its new king.

YORCK
Johann David Ludwig Graf Yorck von Wartenburg (1759 – 1830)

While the butcher Napoleon allowed still more French boys to be slaughtered in the tens of thousands on the frozen steppes of Russia, once hostilities had begun again, an event of historic proportions took place in East Prussia in 1812 when the Prussian general Johann David Ludwig Count Yorck allowed Russians to cross his territory, a treasonous act that horrified Frederick William III but was the catalyst for a groundswell that would see the common man rise up against the French invader. Yorck raised a volunteer army of 20,000, vowing to do or die with honor. Frederick William did finally come around, sending men to Tsar Alexander in view of a joint Russian-Prussian war plan against Napoleon. Napoleon's presence in Germany ended in the Battle of Leipzig in 1813, when more French fathers, sons and brothers were wiped out. Yet French mothers continued to send their sons to Napoleon, weeping with happiness, as did Spartan wives and mothers and sisters, when their boys returned *on* their shields.

CAMBACÉRÈS
1753 – 1824

As Napoleon played an immense role in Prussian history, perhaps we can very briefly touch on the little we know about his homosexuality, as well as that of his aid, Cambacérès, which has its amusing aspects. Jean Jacques Régis de Cambacérès, as first council, had complete powers when Napoleon was on campaign, and he ruled huge regions of Europe while Napoleon was bogged down in Russia. He fully appreciated beautiful boys but didn't raise a finger to stop Napoleon from sending perhaps a million to an early death. Under his supervision the French Civil Law Code was written (and is still in place today), in which we find the article that legalized, in 1791, homosexuality (in that it *de*criminalized sodomy), although most historians accord in saying that the law was especially aimed at undermining Catholicism, Napoleon's way of giving it the Imperial finger. That said, there were laws against offenses to ''public decency'', which allowed the police to handle homosexuals in any way they wished--as those very same laws do today. Cambacérès was openly gay, unheard of for the times.

Cambacérès graduated in law and was an expert accountant. During the Revolution he was part of the Committee of Public Safety during the Reign of Terror and somehow kept his head when Robespierre lost his. A Freemason, he saw to it that 1,200 lodges were created throughout France.

Late for a meeting with Napoleon, he gave, as an excuse, being retained by a lady. ''Well, next time you tell him that a rendezvous with the Emperor is of more importance, and to take his walking stick and his hat and get the hell out.'' (''*Quand on a rendez-vous avec l'Empereur, on dit à ces dames de prendre leurs cannes et leurs chapeaux et de foutre le camp.''* The translation is slightly lame because in French it's obvious that Napoleon is referring to men even if he uses the word *''dames''*, but not that obvious in English if one translates word for word.)

When Talleyrand saw him with two other men he said, in Latin, there goes *haec*, *hic* and *hoc*: she, he and it, the she for **Cambacérès**.

In school in Montpellier, his teacher, seeing him with still another boy, said ''If you continue those vile ways of yours you'll become a pariah, detested by all. (*''Si vous persévérez dans ces pratiques infâmes, vous ne réussirez jamais dans la vie, vous serez un paria, méprisé par tout le monde.''*)

Napoleon told him to at least be *seen* with women, so he took up with a certain lady who became pregnant. When **Cambacérès's** entourage congratulated him, he told them that he had only known her posterior to her pregnancy: *''Non, je ne suis pas le père, je n'ai connu mademoiselle Cuizot que postérieurement.''* In French *postérieurement* means both *afterwards* and the *buttocks*, so although he meant to say that they had met after her pregnancy, it came out that he couldn't be the father because he had had her anally.

Frank Richardson wrote *Napoleon: Bisexual Emperor* in 1973, noting that the emperor chose handsome boys he rapidly promoted. From his exile in St. Helena he wrote that when he saw a handsome boy he felt his ''admiration'' directly in his loins as well as ''in a place I won't name''. The explorer Richard Burton, a homosexual (4), referred to Napoleon's homosexuality in his writings. Brian Joseph Martin in his *Napoleonic Friendship* noted that soldiers who survived his campaigns remained close to each other the rest of their lives. Martin states that the key to such friendships was Napoleon's unique paternal concern for his men. At the time, says Martin, men slept two to a bed in order to save space and to keep warm. When Napoleon noticed that the men's feet often stuck out of the beds he spent a million francs on longer beds, even though he could just as well have spent the money on wider beds or separate beds. For a man as well known as Napoleon it's amazing that we know nothing more on this subject, and that everything stated above is entirely circumstantial.

FREDERICK WILLIAM IV (1795 – 1861)

Prussian nationalism was at an all-time high after the defeat of Napoleon, and to thank his army Frederick William III inaugurated the famous Iron Cross, given to all soldiers, from recruits to generals. Equality went a step further when the king promoted men through the ranks according to their merit and not their birth, a first.

Free of the French tyrant, expectations were now at zenithal levels throughout Europe as peoples sought new freedoms. The Swiss were given a liberal constitution as was Naples. Saxony dismissed its conservative ministers and the new Prussian king Frederick William IV offered his people, who gathered by thousands in Berlin to welcome him, freedom of the press, a new parliament (the Diet), a new constitution and a national flag. The Berliners were wild with joy until an incredible incident occurred. Troops--the best controlled, the most patient and genuinely decided to harm no one--had been stationed in the vicinity when two of their firearms went off accidently, one caught in its owner's saber, the second in an accident as silly. The crowd, unused to military violence of any form (in fact, boys could mercilessly taunt soldiers who themselves would flee!) ran for cover, some climbing onto the roofs and hurling down tiles. The soldiers, bloodied, entered the buildings, mad with indignant rage and slaughtered whoever was at hand. The end result was 100 soldiers and 300 citizens killed.

Frederick William IV then sent out a proclamation begging the people to return home, in exchange for which he gave his word that the army would be ordered out of the city, which is what took place.

The army leader who had had such perfect control over his troops was Ernst von Pfuel, erudite and tolerant, and a friend of Wilhelm von Humboldt. During Pfuel's later career he would become Governor of Berlin, Minister of War and Prime Minister. He opened the world's first military swimming school. He was the lover of novelist and short story writer Bernd Heinrich Wilhelm von Kleist, a boy who lost both parents very young and entered the army, at age 15, to honor his father, a captain, but retired at age 22 to take up literature. His love affaires were with his army comrades, but perhaps because of guilt over his homosexuality his life was one of restless melancholy. Kleist's existing letters to Pfuel mention both his sexual attraction to him from the time he first saw him bathing naked in the Lake of Thun (''your wide shoulders, the curve of your back'') and his gratitude for Pfuel's ''having abused him'' (''I can remember that night in Paris [where they were stationed] when you abused me in such a wondrous manner''). Kleist was a Wagnerian romantic, seemingly torn between masochism and the wish for unspoiled (sexually clean) romanticism. It would appear that he was promiscuous and equated sex with death, in the way that the French call the act of love *la petite mort*. His relationship with men was ever tempestuous, and nonexistent with women, although he ended it all at a lakeside (Thun?) in a suicide pact with a deathly ill woman. He shot her and then himself.

Bernd Heinrich Wilhelm von Kleist by Anton Graff

Another of Pfuel's intimate friends was Frederick Wilhelm Heinrich von Humboldt, geographer, naturalist, explorer, philosopher of romanticism and founder of the University of Berlin. He explored the Amazon and the Orinoco where he collected 60,000 plant species. Humboldt favored young soldiers, writing to one boy, ''No friend could love another as much as I love you, and my only fear is that your impressionable soul may believe that I don't love you as much as you love me.'' To another lad he offered a trip to Switzerland and Sweden, assuring him that he had the money to cover them both (one thousand thalers), stating ''your wishes will be my commands''. To still another, Reinhard, he wrote that Goethe wanted him to drop by, ''but that would mean seeing you six days later which I would not do for anything in the world. I can only be happy in your presence.''

The period known as Romanticism had but one god, one's imagination. Raw feeling counted, as did spontaneity. One did not copy from the works of others (like painters reproducing old masters), which killed originality. Nothing was to be calculated, like Seurat's pointillism or Cezanne's cubism. A connection to nature was healthy. What mattered was one's personal voice and self-assertion. *Romantique* was used in the French sense, not in the English sexual interpretation. The period covered the late 1700s to the mid-1800s.

Frederick William IV had a younger brother who was the opposite of him, a boy fired with testosterone who was so sick of his weak older brother that, tears in his eyes, he threw his sword at Frederick William's feet and marched away. The boy was right in that Frederick William was a maudlin romantic, easy to tears, whose life was based on religion and attempts to understand and tolerate absolutely everyone. To underline this, Frederick William went onto the balcony of his palace and bowed in contrition to the crowds below that had shown up with the corpses of those slain by the troops in the above-mentioned slaughter. His wife, standing next to him, white with shock--whether from fear of the crowd or her husband's humiliation is not known--muttered, Christopher Clark tells us: ''All that's needed now is the guillotine.'' Yet unlike Louis XVI, Frederick William was wildly popular, certainly in part because the people knew he would accord them what they wanted, and in part because he was their fortress against those like his brother who hated common Berliners so much he would have had *their* heads on a platter.

Alas, this wasn't good enough for the most extreme elements of the population. Martial law was therefore declared and 13,000 troops entered Berlin. The same scenario was repeated throughout Germany, bringing temporary calm because although the troops were the most stable and disciplined in history, they were also the most formidable, the reason why no one in his right mind would mess with them (except, again, boys who could even throw stones at them without the slightest fear of reprisal).

Frederick William had promised the Prussians a new flag and they got it, red, black and gold. For a time their was talk of organizing the states around Prussia into a German Reich with Frederick William as its first emperor. This fell through but one wonders, deep down, just who Frederick William was. A case in point was a delegation sent from the state of Frankfurt who came to give him their allegiance in a new united Germany. Frederick William politely refused but he then sent a letter to the Russian Tsar, his sister's husband, telling him that the Frankfurters were dogs and pigs who had nothing to *give* him, although they could have *asked* him to accept.

The period was known for its Romanticism, as stated above, as well as its most world-renowned philosopher, Nietzsche, Prussia's most notorious gift to the world.

PART V

NIETZSCHE
1844 – 1900
AND THE HOMOEROTIC PRUSSIAN ARTISTS VON GLOEDEN AND PLUSCHOW

I discovered the homosexual side of Nietzsche in the excellent *Who's Who in Gay and Lesbian History*, edited by Robert Aldrich and Garry Wotherspoon, and was astonished by the similarities of our shared beliefs, not that I have an iota of his philosophical profundity--it took me a moment to even be able to spell his name correctly--which puts me, intellectually, in my correct place, but that can serve the reader as I've strived to, first, understand his concepts, then to relate them as clearly as possible. Nonetheless, what we have in common, to me, is priceless because his is a veritable intellect. Neither of us believed/believes in a god, a principle I laid down in my book *BOYS, 3000 Years of Love between Men*: ''Education, Xenophon hammered again and again, was the key to male love. Mutual education. And sharing. The transfer of qualities. The need of bodily contact. Of bodily love. Of shared release. This hunger for knowledge, so brilliantly and thrillingly continued by da Vinci, must go on: The time has come for us to accept responsibility for our acts, accept that voodoo superstitions and gods are no longer indispensable. Today we must let our children freely choose their sexuality and place them in an ambience, male and female, which will ensure that choice. We must cease disfiguring them physically with circumcision and disfiguring them mentally with religious hocus-pocus. We must introduce them to the heroes that have fashioned our lives and made progress possible--the very essence of this book--true heroes, not comic-book surrogates.'' From the very beginning of time to the beheadings of our own enlightened days men--who have been too weak to stand of their own feet to face their own destinies though the force of their own shoulders and their powers of reasoning--have destroyed life in the name of some god. From the still-beating hearts of lads, torn from their chests--hundreds of thousands, perhaps even millions, at the hands of the Aztecs and Incas--down to Richard I who put 2,400 Muslims to the sword before the walls of Jerusalem itself. There were the 8,000 boys age 13 and over murdered at Srebrenica, and, again, the televised slitting of throats described, but mercifully not shown, nearly weekly on CNN. Nietzsche and I also share an illogical admiration for Cesare Borgia--illogically because he was a psychopathic killer--about whom I wrote *Cesare Borgia: His Violent Life, His Violent Times*.

At the age of 17, *seventeen*, Nietzsche was giving vent to ideas that would form the basis of French existentialism, especially in his declaration that ''Man is condemned to be free,'' a feeling of hope and promise at the time that has certainly not been fulfilled, as the Germans went on to choose Hitler, Spain a king, England the continuation of royalty, and the Arab Spring ended in worse dictatorships still, and worse slaughter.

Also at age 17 he wrote, ''That God should have become a man indicates only that man must not seek his salvation in infinity--his heaven is on earth. Only through grave doubts and battles does mankind become manly.''

And the lad goes on, ''God, the immortality of the soul, redemption, the 'beyond' were concepts I had no time to pay attention to--not even as a child, perhaps because I wasn't childish enough. I was too curious, too questioning, too exuberant to put up with a concept as crude as the existence of a god. For me, God was an invitation *to not think*." Whoever put it better than that?

Truly active human beings, Nietzsche went on to say, no longer take Christianity seriously, while middle-class intellectuals have watered down its interdictions to a kind of soft moralism, turning their backs on biblical Abrahams who would sacrifice biblical Isaacs, beliefs in a vengeful god that nonetheless spanned thousands of years. The comic aspect of human existence is that even the greatest of us slide back into obscurantism. Socrates, overcoming sickness, tells his servant that he owes the sacrifice of a cock to the mythological physician Asclepius in thanks for his recovery, proof that even he was superstitious. Hadrian may have ordered Antinous' drowning in the superstitious belief that the years left to the boy would be added to his own life (6).

Royalty, says Nietzsche, is the supreme right of the few over the supreme right of the many. It is the superiority by birthright of those who lord it over others simply because they have the outside trappings of nobility, which sets them apart from the rest of mankind. Royalty is an invitation to the herd to let their betters do all the thinking (and its corollary, amass all the wealth), a form of obscurantism against which Nietzsche ceaselessly waged war, on behalf of science and the freeing of the mind.

As my reading into the life of Nietzsche began to deepen, I became aware that I was far from alone, not only in my difficulty in understanding the depth of his thinking, but even in comprehending the most mundane aspects of his life. His homosexuality, for example, of prime interest to me in my quest to prove that gay genius has contributed as much to the betterment of the world as has straight genius--a point brought home by the existence of a single man, for me the greatest to have walked the earth, Leonardo da Vinci. Joachim Köhler wrote a whole book on Nietzsche's homosexuality: *Zarathustra's Secret. The Interior Life of Friedrich Nietzsche.* There's not a shred of evidence of his being gay, although Köhler tried to prove otherwise. The boys he went on holiday with, who visited him for more or less long periods in Genoa, Nice, Sicily, Sils Maria near St. Moritz in Switzerland, Turin and Rapallo could have been no more than pals. Even the recurrent name of Paul Rée as his paramour means little, as we all have best friends with whom we take great non-sexual pleasure in frequenting, and even some homo-hating Australians would die for their mates, yet the weight of circumstantial evidence leaves little doubt of his inner homosexual nature.

On Sicily he spent time at Taormina, a village used to seeing Englishmen and Germans. The lads flocked to the beaches, intercepted the men in the narrow streets, and in the rocks, perfectly naked. The lads not only sported boners but enacted in the men's view what they did together or in groups in private from puberty onwards, only now they would be paid by the salivating boy-lovers who literally worshipped their charms. Had Nietzsche let them have their way with him? What man could have resisted?

Sicilian boys by Wilhelm von Gloeden

Wilhelm von Gloeden had gone to the island of Sicily for his health. His guide was a 16-year-old donkey driver with whom he spent a night in such ecstasy, he wrote, that he bought a villa and hired local 13- and 14-year-olds to staff it. The boys' parents competed in having their lads work for him as he paid well, he took scrupulous care of their health and needs, he turned over the royalties from the photos he took of them, and he provided dowries so that his favorites could marry. His character was such that everyone sought him out. His orgies became famous and visitors to them were said to have been in the hundreds (presumably not all at the same time). Frederick von Krupp was one, who later tried to recreate Taormina on Capri. Gloeden was noted as the first man to use filters and body make-up, said to have been composed of milk, glycerin, olive oil and perfume. He left his negatives to his lover, Il Moro, whom he had ''known'' at age 13. He at times worked with his cousin, Guglielmo Plüschow, an avid boy-lover said to have been less talented and more stilted in his posing of the lads. Some people at Taormina, today, claim that the origin of their wealth is a heritage from the sums given to their grandsons.

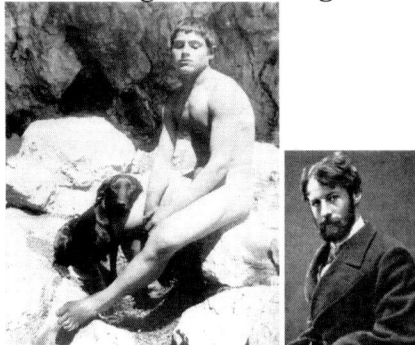

Il Moro and Gloeden

The universe into which Nietzsche was born was wonderfully idyllic. He saw first light near Leipzig. The towns and villages of his youth all had beautiful steepled slate-covered roofs, small-paned windows and chimney tops emitting grey to black smoke in thick masses, as inside the homes the fireplaces were working overtime in the dreadful winters. Summers were no less idyllic, green meadows that surrounded ponds and lakes of perfect purity, adorned, in painting after painting, by naked lads frolicking, showing off and laughing, and there is no music as wondrous as a boy's laugher. That said, the cities at the time, in Germany, France and England, were filthy with horse and human feces, along with ever-present diseases like cholera. The same was especially true in Berlin which would nonetheless become, in a few short years, the cleanest city in the western world, with bathhouses and a plethora of public toilets. Nietzsche's parents were educated and the only shadow on his youth was the loss of his father to brain damage at age 44. Nietzsche took to music, writing compositions of his own, even symphonies and, later, an oratorio. He learned to ride expertly in a volunteer cadet program, but was so severely injured when falling against the pommel of his saddle that he had to give up all thought of a military career. He was an excellent student, especially good in literature and languages, less so in mathematics. He had friends, he went to beer taverns where he drank stein for stein. He liked dances, was often in debt, and voiced the right of every student to sow a few wild oats. At age 22 he came down with syphilis that some historians believe he contracted in a male whorehouse in Genoa. Others suggest he died a virgin, while still others say that it was just as possible that he stepped outside taverns during drinking bouts to piss in nearby parks, offering himself to anyone, from a fellow student to an older man, taking and giving pleasure, all in a matter of minutes, as this was homosexual sex at the time, as it is today, as I well know from having lived and loved in Germany. At the time there was no Germany as such, but sex among the Prussians, especially in the army, was current money, as the French say. His personal life was even more hermetic than his writing, which is saying a lot.

Nietzsche

Later in his life one of his doctors stated that he had told Nietzsche to have intercourse as a way of lessening stress, and that Nietzsche had done so.

At age 17, perhaps influenced by Cartesian France and anti-clerical Voltaire, he had an epiphany: the existence of a god and the immortality of the soul were based exclusively on faith. They were assumptions impossible to prove. Suppositions he was no longer ready to blindly accept. ''The Truth is always Difficult,'' he wrote, and ''if you aspire to peace and happiness, then believe; if you want the Truth, then you must search.''

At age 18 he still slavishly gave himself up to student concerns, drinking himself under the table at fests, giving as well as taking in student duels where he exchanged a scar on his nose for one he gave another boy on his forehead. Never a looker, he was short, short-sighted and corpulent, a natty dresser thanks to his mother who lived with her mother and two of her late husband's sisters, the sources of Nietzsche's money. He was already suffering from physical disabilities that would plague him throughout his life, ever increasing in severity, until one of them killed him: chronic digestive problems, increasingly chronic headaches, bad teeth and rheumatism, for which he took great quantities of opium.

At age 21 he fell in love with Schopenhauer whom he never met but followed with dog-like servility. He excelled in his studies to such an extent that a paper he handed in on Theognis won him accolades from his teacher who was instrumental in seeing that he was given, at age 24, the Chair of Classical Philology at the University of Basel, before he even received his doctorate. His lifestyle as a student consisted of morning lectures, lunch at the excellent Mahn's restaurant, coffee at the Café Kintschy where he and friends skimmed through newspapers, nightly drinking at the Weinstube, and meetings of his Philological Club. He was impeccably dressed, in fact dressing like a man three times his age.

The basis of Schopenhauer's work is that the world is driven by a continually dissatisfied will and that the only way not to be dissatisfied is by asceticism and chastity. He easily admitted to having been influenced by Vedantic and Buddhist thinking. Life involves suffering and suffering is caused by desire; the extinction of desire leads to liberation. Suffering is caused by desire for more. Men are motivated exclusively by their own basic desires; desires that are, he says, futile, illogical and directionless. ''A man can do what he wants but he cannot will what he wants.'' People cannot improve, he believed. Moral reform is impossible and can only be controlled by stiff penalties. Punishment must be a greater motive to not commit a crime than the motive to do wrong. He believed capital punishment was an absolute necessity.

He was an atheist who taught that ''the world is itself the Last Judgment.'' He was in no way aesthetic himself and freely admitted that it was unnecessary for a philosopher to be a saint, as it is for a saint to be a philosopher. One doesn't have to be beautiful in order to create beautiful art, the example being Michelangelo.

Some thumbnails into is beliefs:

Marriage leads to halving one's rights and doubling one's duties. It's like putting a hand in a sack, hoping to come up with an eel and not a snake.

Music is the highest form of life and a temporary way of escaping pain.

The white race is superior thanks to climate. In going north blacks became white while their intellectual and inventive powers increased thanks to the challenges offered by the increasingly colder climate. He did make exceptions for Indians and Egyptians.

Perhaps the most misogynist of all philosophers, he wrote that women make perfect elementary and nursery teachers because they are ''childish, frivolous and short-sighted'' as are their pupils. But he did add that a woman who could raise herself higher than the masses had more potentiality than men.

Men of intelligence and nobility should be given a harem, while the others should be castrated. A new Periclean Age would then arise.

A good person can be spotted by his kindness to animals.

Who would want to become an esthetic, to not want the love of another, knowing that such a love would lead to inevitable suffering, as it has in my own case, always, without exception. But it is that love and that suffering, and the hope of more love, despite the consequences, that defines me. Otherwise, why not be just a vegetable?

He fell in love too with Erwin Rohde, with whom he would travel over many years. Both were brought together by their devotion of Schopenhauer.

At age 22, as said, he contracted syphilis. One author, Curtis Cate in his extremely complete *Friedrich Nietzsche*, suggested it occurred when he and his friends "took the edge off their adolescent lust" by frequenting a heterosexual whorehouse. This would not have been an exceptional divertissement even for someone with homosexual tendencies. Prussian soldiers were known for their orgies, the homosexual element deeply stirred by the presence of the naked bodies of their heterosexual comrades in the act of copulation.

The first period of his life, the foundation of his education, took place at the renowned Schulpforta *Gymnasium* (German for High School), reserved for brilliant students then as today, where he not only composed music and wrote plays and poetry, he also began his own autobiography. He did humanistic studies and studies in classical language and philology. This led to works on Homer and his first two books, *The Birth of Tragedy* and *The Untimely Mediations*, both motivated by his reaction to Schopenhauer, and both an emotive reaction to the extreme influence of Wagner who was the same age as his father, and who had welcomed Nietzsche as a son. During this period he gave lectures and wrote on philosophy during the age of the Greeks, concentrating on pre-Platonic philosophers who had been responsible for an age in which men could realize themselves thanks to competitions in the creation of plays, festivals of music, politics in the agora, athletic contests--a perfect climate in which men could develop into perfect orchids. At the end of this period he struck out on his own after leaving the University of Basel. The University had grown tired of his absences due to recurrent illness and his megalomania. Nietzsche had grown so larger-than-life in his own eyes that even the professor who had made his entrance into the University possible, Ritschl, gave up on him.

Köhler in his *Zarathustra's Secret* offers us a very beautiful story concerning Nietzsche and a boy he met during a conference, whom he invited back to his rooms. Nietzsche served tea and a conversation began, at one point including the boy's impressions of a sketch attributed to Hans Holbein. Which of the two, the man, 24, or the boy, 17, brought up the subject is unknown but the boy had liked the picture and had tried to explain just why. The boy himself tells the story: "I strove in vain to find words to describe the magical attraction of the wonderful portrait. Words failed me. I saw the lips before my eyes--full and succulent. 'Lips,' I stammered, helplessly, 'made for ...' " And from the corner of the room came Nietzsche's soft voice: " 'made for kissing.' " Only later, continued Köhler, did the boy know that Nietzsche had uttered a confession.

Holbein's self-portrait.

His contacts with his students varies from one biographer to another. He's said to have found them "stupid young men", yet he was supposedly adored, one pupil going so far as to leaving him violets on his desk and drawing a heart on the blackboard. He often invited them to his rooms in which they were very politely received and put at ease by his kindness. Yet others berated his exaggerated intensity, his high-blown manner, and one added he couldn't even fart like an everyday man.

During this period he traveled a great deal with Rohde, and planned to build a monastic community with him, devoted to artists and thinkers. Alas, Rohde would later marry, leaving Nietzsche high and dry, one of the greatest deceptions of his life.

During the second, middle period of his life, Nietzsche freed himself from Schopenhauer and Wagner and concentrated on a man's realizing himself, his "becoming what he is" by rising above the herd and imposing his own morality on others, being good when it served his advancement, bad when it fulfilled his needs--the perfect Machiavelli--and by giving free rein to his instincts and cognitive faculties. During this period he wrote *Human, All Too Human.*

In the last period of his life his oeuvre is so opaque that I truly mourn a student obliged to make sense out of the gibberish in order to get a good mark in Philosophy 101 (obviously my personal, uneducated evaluation). For the herd, he maintained, human freedom is a negative *freedom from* restraints and expectations, leaving man free to appreciate football on Sunday t.v., while for the elite freedom is positive, it is *freedom to* achieve, to master oneself. In this period he wrote *Ecce homo*, or How One Becomes What One Is. *Good* is whatever heightens a man's power, whatever enforces his will to power; *bad* is whatever stems from weakness; *happiness* comes when one feels himself to be on the road to increased powers. It was during this third period of his life that he wrote some of his most enigmatic works, works both contentious and, deemed some, unworthy of serious reflection, themes centered around nihilism: *Thus Spoke Zarathustra* in four parts, *The Anti-Christ*, *The Twilight of the Idols*, and a huge amount of material not published until after--sometimes well after--his death, works known as the *Nachlass*.

The name Zarathustra comes from the philosophy taught by a Mede, ancestors of today's Kurds, living in Persia, who sought to bring order out of the chaos of the literally millions of Hindu gods. His Apollo--his God of Light--was Ahura, who cast from heaven the God of Darkness. Nietzsche was attracted to Zarathustra because he had, like Nietzsche himself, turned his back on all but the search for wisdom, and Zarathustra was hated by those around him, as was Nietzsche by religious--Protestant and Catholic--fanatics. Because so little was known about Zarathustra, who lived around 700 B.C., Nietzsche could place whatever he wanted in his mouth. Nietzsche, like Zarathustra, like Siddhartha, had spent ten years in solitary thought, and in fact said that he, Nietzsche, had been the same age as Zarathustra when he ended his isolation at age 39.

Nietzsche agreed with Freud that the fuel of mental and spiritual life was one's sexual nature, so different from Marx for whom the fuel was based on economic needs. Nietzsche believed that there was no pure, abstract reasoning, that, on the contrary, everything was based on ever-changing interests, needs and passions, including sexual pleasure. Nietzsche was said to have been good company, beguiling, ironic, at times scathing, at times touchingly unsure of himself.

The winner in life's lottery, for Nietzsche, is he who follows Pindar's affirmation: Be yourself. A man must follow his inner law, moral when it served him, immoral when needed. Morality was fine for the masses, as were religious beliefs and slave-like acquiescence to their betters, the nobility. Equality, we all know, is non-existent, even among twins. The accident of birth places some of us in Europe, others in Somalia. There are those born with rapid synapses, and those with an I.Q. that leads to the idiocy of the 90% of televised junk the masses watch. There is the tyranny of beauty, those with the facial perfection of *David*. Being born with a silver spoon in the mouth can go a long way in one's success, as can ambition and optimism, two quasi-innate American traits. Nietzsche seems not to have preferred a master over a slave, but he did prefer he who sought to become something, who shucked the ''peace and happiness of Believers in favor of the difficult Route to the Truth, and those who chose it.'' He favored Frost's ''Two roads diverged in a wood, and I--I took the one less traveled by, And that has made all the difference.''

In the absence of a god there is but the outer space of nihilism, nothing to believe in, nothing to give purpose to life. Without a god to cling to men can no longer orient themselves through the shoals of good and evil. Yet in today's world where people, especially Americans, give lip service to religious beliefs, men go their ways without a thought to divine justice, so concerned are they with the justice of men and the courts of law that have the power to imprison them. Their lip service to religion is a kind of after-life insurance policy: one proclaims one's faith just in case there *is* a hereafter. And then, in time of need, how comforting it is to fall to one's knees in search of compassion and understanding. And when one survives a trauma--a fire or automobile accident--what inner peace knowing that His invisible hand had played a role in one's survival, and was even now shielding one with His omnipotence.

Nietzsche was deeply marked by Schopenhauer's nihilism, an evaluation that states that the world should *not* be what it is, and that the world that should be, doesn't exist. That our very existence has no meaning. All of which is true, which leads one to one's first existential decision: to live life anyway, or to kill one's self. To find a reason to go on, outside of religious hocus-pocus, is the challenge, especially as we know the finality will be that of Sisyphus, eternally rolling a stone up a hill, a stone that will eternally roll back to where it had set out. As stated before, Schopenhauer claimed that music was a compensation, the expression of the essence of life, and it's true that music does offer moments of carefree bliss.

Of natural interest is Nietzsche's Superman. It's difficult to know how seriously to take him, in this and other things. He writes that a full-blooded man wants but two things, danger and play--women being the plaything. Men should therefore be educated for engaging in warfare, women for the relaxation of the warrior. ''Everything else is folly,'' he assures us. Of equal silliness is his conception of death: ''Some die too early. Others too late. Die at the right time!'' teaches Zarathustra.

Concerning the Superman: man is but a link between the ape and the Superman, says Nietzsche, a kind of rope over an abyss, and the good news is that man is the bridge than can span the abyss, and not an end in itself. Man is pathetic to the Superman as an ape is an evolutionary embarrassment to man. The Superman rises above morality and notions of good and evil, and those who do not attain him remain men, the herd. The herd has no great passions, commitments and dreams, it earns its living, avoids crisis, the unknown, in order to eat and keep itself warm.

To me it's amusing to note the number of people who shake their heads at Nietzsche's pessimism. He spoke of the decline of the human species but I'm certain he never envisaged the cremation of 6 million of them in his own Germany. He regretted the drop in intellectual curiosity, but he could not have foreseen today's press, written for the intellectual level of a 13-year-old, and as for television, who could have foretold fraudulent quiz shows, scenes of fucking in legitimate films, and the Wheel of Fortune? No one of even my generation could have predicted the possibility of mass beheadings and children sent out as human bombs.

In my mind, as a student, Nietzsche was a thundering personage roaming the world as big and powerful as Paul Bunyan, as mighty as club-swinging Heracles. The opposite of the short, corpulent, walrus-mustached, physically-frail creature eternally feuding with his sister. Yet he wrote, ''Believe me when I affirm that the secret to fulfillment and the greatest possible thrill found in existence come through living dangerously!'' As far as I can see, there was not one instance of danger in his entire life.

He was deeply influenced by Dostoevsky, and he deeply influenced my favorite composer Mahler, as well as the Japanese writer-weight-lifter-Superman Mishima, whose suicide made his reputation and froze in time his gym-maintained beauty (when he visited N.Y. Mishima would invariably ask Capote, perhaps America's greatest writer, to provide him with boys with big cocks, which infuriated Capote who would cry out, ''Why do they all think I have access to boys with big cocks!?!'').

His health began degrading rapidly, and in addition to the usual problems linked to age, he suffered from nausea and headaches, vomiting, and from nervous seizures--reoccurring at ever-shorter intervals. An admirer of his works, Paul Lanzky, invited Nietzsche to a hotel he ran near Florence. There Nietzsche found a letter from his sister suggesting some medicines he might take. In answer he lectured her on the age in which they lived, an age of unmanly, weak self-seekers, and extolled Shakespeare for his characters, men of iron, rough, hard, made of granite.

At age 41 he published *Beyond Good and Evil*, in which the reader is encouraged to rise above notions of what is true/false, good/bad, beautiful/ugly, useful/useless, black/white and enter a world of colors and tonalities, refusing doglike servitude to anything or anyone. He now claimed that what drove people was the will to power, and that Darwin was mistaken in believing it to be the need for self-preservation. Along with the will to power comes the will to obey, without which there would be chaos, a function naturally reserved for the ''herd''.

He extended his views on women, stating, incredibly, that men were destroying women's femininity by giving them an education, by encouraging them to make decisions, to read newspapers, and have political opinions. An obscurantism that exists to this very day, and even in modern Greece Jacky Onassis was outraged when, during a friendly get-together with her new husband and her husband's male friends, she voiced a political opinion and was told to shut up. The resulting fireworks were said to have been gargantuan. As for Nietzsche, he claimed that higher societies were always based on a form of slavery, as was ancient Greece, and that women were there to obey, in return for which men offered their protection and, he wrote, ''spared them''.

Most males got off hardly better. Without going into the reasons why, Nietzsche predicted that the current tendency to democratize society would produce a new race of minimally educated, hard-working men who would follow the orders given by an exceptional Supermen, because in every generation there are always a few, a Frederick the Great here, a Napoleon there. Whatever the roots of such a hypothesis, the prediction did come true, and a path opened for the likes of Stalin, Hitler and Mussolini.

Once, in one of my classes, a student--who happened to be Greek--declared that slavery was as prevalent today as during the times of his ancestors. I laughed and asked him to tell the students around the table who these current slaves were. Without saying a word, he looked at each and every one of us.

Supermen vanquish thanks to hardships. Like the Spartans who bathed their babies in ice-cold cascades, only the fittest survived. It is in the weak classes, today's slaves, that one finds morality, compassion, humility and patience. The weak classes that believe in the Christian promise of escape from a cruel and unsatisfactory world into an imaginary afterlife of eternal bliss.

Nietzsche wrote that religions have poisoned man's existence from their very origin, except for the Greeks who had created an Olympian godhead that had as many foibles as does man himself. Zeus and Hera were in continual conflict, as were their earthling counterparts. Dionysus favored girls while Apollo coveted boys. The Olympians forgave men's actions not because they were sinful but because they were foolish, and no one was more foolish than the gods themselves. Religions that came afterwards developed the notion of sin, making even the earth a source of such sinfulness that the only escape was renunciation of earthly pleasures in favor of all-forgiving heaven. The road to salvation passed through God, for only He could forgive sin. Thanks to God, a man's conscience could find relief. Nietzsche put this conscience-vivisection on a par with animal-vivisection, or man's cruelty to animals. Only a Superman could save men from such nonsense, which has enchained men since Adam. This would happen through the coming of a new Messiah, and Nietzsche was certain that such a man was on his way.

At age 44 he came out with his *Ecce homo*, an autobiography with chapter titles such as Why I am so Wise, Why I am so Clever, Why I write such Good Books, in which Nietzsche offered a list of his illnesses, confessed that he wrote about Wagner and Schopenhauer as a means of writing about himself, and admitted that he would prefer to be considered a satyr than a saint. His desire was to run with the beautiful and healthy, something that neither his inner being nor outer body would have permitted. The title,

Ecce homo, comes from the presentation of Pontius Pilate of Christ to his Jewish accusers. "Here is the man." He stresses his hatred of Germany, its terrible weather, riffraff population, and suggested that even Wagner would not have realized himself had he not gone on to live in Paris. Nietzsche wanted his book translated simultaneously into several languages, 1,000 copies for brutish Germany, incapable of understanding "his lofty style", to 300,000 for the French. This was not proof of his incipient madness, it represented Nietzsche's sincere evaluation of himself, one reinforced by a very select group of admirers. And why not? What was left unsold then (the vast majority of his printings) has indeed sold out since.

Or *was* it the onset of illness? For he began writing letters to his friends claiming that in past lives he had been Buddha, Alexander the Great, Napoleon, Caesar and others. He signed them The Crucified One. He wrote letters to the King and Queen of Italy that the hotel keeper quietly stashed away, and then he fell at the hooves of a horse that was being beaten by its owner, attempting to save it, and entered a coma, from which he immerged insane.

Do we need to know more? Once the mind is gone all is gone. Asylums, care at the hands of his mother, care at those of his sister. His death. His incineration. His Augustan assent into the Heaven of Immortal Philosophers.

OTTO VON BISMARCK (1815 – 1898)
WILHELM (WILLIAM) II (1888 – 1918)

Bismarck was a masterful manipulator whose good luck was having a king under his thumb, William I (who followed Frederick William III), and an excellent army under good generals who knew how to take advantage of innovations in weaponry, especially cannons.

Bismarck reigned supreme for 30 years, a master at diplomatic chess and a master at keeping the peace, despite his often-maligned reputation. Biographers have defined him as polite, witty and charming, brutal, deceitful and disarmingly honest.

He presided over battles against Denmark, Austria and France, then ruled by Napoleon III. Thanks to the guidance of Bismarck, Prussians not only defeated Napoleon but took him prisoner. At a peace signed at Versailles William I's son Wilhelm II was declared emperor of a Germany Bismarck had succeeded in uniting. The year of German unification was 1871.

The British immediately understood the importance of the new German entity, as did the Austrians who inaugurated an alliance with Bismarck that swept away centuries of hatred between the two countries, one that lasted right up to Hitler's anschluss. But a major grain of dissent had been sown in 1870 when Bismarck took Alsace-Lorraine from Napoleon III, laying the foundation for the war of 1914 – 1918, during the last days of which the last German monarch, Wilhelm II, abdicated and sought shelter in the Netherlands. The Allies' revenge for the war of 1914 – 1918, (WWI), took place in the Hall of Mirrors, the same room where German unification had come into being. Their draconian, punitive demands would lead to WWII.

The havoc after 1918 in Germany was horrifying, with strikes, continuous violence and the extreme left seeking power. In the month of March 1919 alone, 1,200 Germans died when troops battled communists in open revolt, firing at them with machine guns, cannons and flame-throwers.

Miraculously the political parties came together in 1920 to form a constitution that bestowed sovereignty on the German people. Bureaucratic jobs and the highest positions in the military now went to commoners, sons and daughters of factory workers and farmers.

THE WEIMAR REPUBLIC (1919 – 1933)

The Weimar Republic replaced the German Empire in 1919. It was named Weimar after the city where it was constitutionally created, although its official name was the German Reich. It was a success in that it renegotiated the terms of the Treaty of Versailles so that Germany paid few of the war reparations demanded of it. Lubricity in Weimar was unbridled and omnisexual. It was homoerotic, ephebophile and sadomasochistic. Like Berlin today, and Sans Francisco, everything went, and a boy--a schoolboy--could earn a living as soon as he was old enough to understand what was going on around him. Soldiers too could round off their wages by fucking the likes of the writer Christopher Isherwood and the poet W.H. Auden, whose chapter follows. Boys could be butch. Historian Louis Snyder claimed that Röhm believed homosexuals could outdo straights in brawls, killing "and slaughtering for the hell of it". Historian Thomas Tuchs wrote that Hitler himself felt that homosexuals were second to none when it came to "beating up anyone opposed to Nazis". This was very bad publicity for homosexuals because, for the first time, the public became aware that they could be dangerous. Yet in reality homosexuality took the opposite form, as cross-dressing was in vogue.

What took place in Berlin preceded San Francisco to such an extent that homosexuality was said to have originated there, at least since the Dark Ages of male sexuality that followed the Christianization of Ancient Rome.

PART VI

THE ORIGIN OF HOMOSEXUALITY

What is amazing in the history of love among males was that after the Renaissance there followed an age darker than the Middle Ages which had preceded the Renaissance. Love between males during the Renaissance could be punished by death, but in reality under Lorenzo *Il Magnifico* de' Medici one got off easily because everyone was doing it, sharing, at some point in their lives, an orgasm with another male. As girls were worth their weight in gold thanks to advantageous marriages that would enrich their husbands, they were kept locked away. Unlike a boy who could offer himself to a hundred passing hands or mouths or anuses and still claim innocence, a girl had one chance, after which the fruit was eternally spoiled.

After the Renaissance we stepped back into the dark, where lads, in the 1800s, could not comprehend their attraction to lads, those they had seen swimming in rivers and lakes, naked and so beautiful the boys dreaming of them inundated their own bellies in equally wondrous rivers and lakes. Till then, men were thought (by some) to have become homosexual because they were so insatiable sexually that they simply turned to men as an alternative to women who now bored them. Sexuality was malleable, and one could alter it at will. To keep boys on the right track laws were harsh, although thankfully the death penalty had been dropped, except, in one of life's never-ending paradoxes, in Berlin--until 1868. It was felt that men who cared for other men were in reality women trapped in a man's body, which would not only account for their searching out other men, but would account too for those who were effeminate. The woman within was seeking an outlet for her femininity.

Men who were lucky, mostly educated men who emigrated to Berlin, could find sexual satisfaction in the garrison city of 400,000 where soldiers padded their pay by selling themselves, and that for generations. The unlucky ones, the vast majority, may have felt that they and their sexuality were alone in the world, that no others shared their dreams and lust. These would live and die alone. Following the French Revolution laws against sodomy were abolished in France in 1791, as reported. Under French influence they were abolished also in Spain, Belgium, the Netherlands and Italy. Certain parts of Germany followed. In Bavaria, for example, only those who raped other men or who had sex with boys under 12 were prosecuted. But in all parts of Germany men could be imprisoned if they did something against public decency, a seemingly normal demand since having sex, for example, in the middle of a public street (homosexual or heterosexual sex), struck everyone as bad form. The law, in reality however, was diverted to cover whatever the police wanted it to cover. An example: a boy who related to another boy how he had been fucked--but well paid--in a park, was overheard by a woman who was shocked, a public act of indecency because the boys had spoken in public. The boy was found and jailed. But even this liberalism was revoked following several horrendous rapes of minors, and in 1871 laws were again reenacted in Germany against sodomy.

The population of Berlin exploded, from the 400,000 to 4 million in 1920. Berlin went from a city of open sewers to the first city ever electrified, with, in 1800, electric streetcars and lighting. It went from a city of open sewers to one of public toilets and baths, from the filthiest to the cleanest city in the world, infinitely more hygienic than London, Paris and N.Y. At the end of the 1400s in Florence the Office of the Night was formed to put an end to sodomy. The penalty was death but everyone got off with a slap on the wrist, except those who forced children to have sex. In 1885 Berlin established the Department of Homosexuals, proof of the growing number of gays. The police collected information and mug shots of homosexuals, and encouraged doctors and educators to study Berlin's unique sexual subculture, thanks to which reams of information concerning the sexuality of the times have come to us. In 1896 the name of the Department of Homosexuals was changed to Department of Homosexuals and Blackmailers. More money could be gained by pimps putting 14-year-old boys on the streets and then blackmailing the clients. In 1902 Friedrich Alfred Krupp, the Cannon King, committed suicide when blackmail led to the publication of his preference for Italian boys. For such a rich, powerful man to end his own life so young spoke volumes about being branded a homosexual, about the prevalence of blackmail and about the availability of underage lads. The department store magnate Hermann Israel killed himself on his yacht at age 40 when his companion blackmailed him. Before dying Israel turned the boy's threatening letters over to the police. The lad was sentenced to two months imprisonment. Victims of blackmail numbered in the hundreds, two of whom were well-known jurists, one who shot his blackmailer when he literally didn't have a cent left to pay him off. In 1902 a 28-year-old ophthalmologist committed suicide when his card was found in a boy's jacket and the ophthalmologist was threatened with a trial. At the time, it was established that a third of Berlin's homosexuals were being blackmailed. But as Berlin's reputation for male prostitution bloomed, johns from all over Europe flocked to the world's greatest center of boys.

Although boy whorehouses would number in the hundreds in the pre-WWI years of Christopher Isherwood, the beginnings in the very early 1900s were rudimentary, where everyone from a club owner to a tobacconist could use a backroom for financial gain, recruiting hustlers and male trade from off the streets. Any man could have a room and rent out his boys, as pimps have since the beginning of time. And as the boys were often twelve to fifteen, their suitors could be either blackmailed or robbed while busy with their young prey. Any schoolboy or shop boy, any servant or thief, sailor or soldier, could round off monthly earnings by playing innocent or butch or changing into drag.

Rich men like Friedrich Alfred Krupp, as stated, were openly blackmailed, or writers would threaten to publish tell-all books if they didn't pay up. Some hustlers trailed likely johns and then, catching hold of them, accused them of soliciting and threatened to call the police. Robert Beachy in his wonderful *Gay Berlin* (2014) tells us that this at times ended in jail terms for the blackmailer, and the boys could be clobbered by the men they pursued, especially if, as in one case, the target was a bullish butcher, but these brave citizens were most probably the vast minority.

What happened next was pretty much inexplicable to rationalists. As clubs gained in number so did those who took advantage of johns, robbing and blackmailing them. More and more targets were out-of-town Germans (city dwellers became streetwise), many well-off merchants and industrialists. This in turn inspired more boys to go to Berlin, which in turn drew still more men seeking youths. Soon the British came, followed by Americans. Those who sought and bought sex returned home to flaunt the merits of Berlin's boys, often hung, often highly-sexed lads who, because of their growing numbers, cost less and less. The minority of men robbed and otherwise extorted turned more and more to the police who had such complete files on the boys, largely thanks to the effective Chief of Police Leopold von Meerscheidt-Hüllessem, that the lads were often apprehended and the stolen goods retrieved. This made great copy for newspapers, thanks to which more and more foreigners learned about Berlin's boys. More rent and johns flocked to the new gay oasis, in (small) part responsible for its population exploding to 4 million, including (according to one estimate) a pre-WWI total of 170 boy bordellos. More than an oasis, Berlin became an earthly heaven because every variation of sex was represented, because beer and liquor flowed, and because of hugely successful floorshows, as seen in Isherwood's *Cabaret*. (Of course, bar hopping and boy hopping can be great fun, but let us not forget that this had as much to do with the blue skies and healthy lads of Ancient Greece as a pigsty to a field of golden wheat.)

That said, many German boys practiced sports that kept their bodies trim, and naked sunbathing took place around lakes, along rivers and even in public swimming pools, thanks to which the boys were beautifully tanned. Many foreign lads, especially the English, the opposite of this, hestitated to denude themselves. Yet sex at the time was so free that one of them, Stephen Spender, at first unwilling to expose his physique, soon found himself at home in Berlin, and as far as love was concerned, ''all one had to do was undress''. German boys tended to be masculine, they liked to exercise and they liked to show off their toned bodies. Their smiles were often ravaging, they enjoyed roughhousing, and sexually were highly experienced. Compared to the English they were animals, studs to British boarding-school lads who were used to lying on their stomachs in wait of the thrill of penetration, something many boys beg for. Of his intimate friend Pieps, Auden said, ''I like sex and Pieps likes money. It's a good exchange.''

Men and youths caught breaking Paragraph 175 got off with a minimal fine or a few days behind bars although blackmailers were imprisoned, one of whom got ten years. But as Beachy points out, between 1904 and 1920 only *two men* were caught in *flagrante delicto* and tried under the accursed Paragraph!

Kiosks were literally flooded with dozens of publications, and the kiosk owners didn't hesitate to have some pinned open, showing nude males. In 1930 Berlin had 280,000 tourists a year, among which were 40,000 Americans. There were believed to have been 100,000 rent-boys, all out for money to live on or pocket change, 1/3rd were believed to have been heterosexual. And they were cheap, especially soldiers and sailors going for 50 pfennig. Thomas Mann discovered Berlin at age 17. Christopher Isherwood refused to spend more than 10 marks, dinner and a few drinks for his boys (although this was outrageously overpaying), W.H. Auden, in his diary, detailed his sexual encounters, and the architect Philip Johnson claimed to have learned German through the horizontal method.

Auden, Spender and Isherwood

Isherwood and a friend.

Neither minors nor anyone badly dressed were admitted to the clubs in west Berlin, called the West End. In the East End everyone could enter. Sex was tame in some high-class clubs (although no-holds-barred was the rule in boy whorehouses). At the urinals boys flashed their wares, and at tables boys allowed johns to put their hands through their pockets, which had been cut away inside to allow seizure of the lads' dicks. Lederhosen was popular in the butch places Isherwood frequented, showing off boys' suntanned thighs. Isherwood was said to have had 500 during the time he was there, from 1929 to 1933. Today, boys can do that in a year, easily, but here we're talking about quantity. Quality is a completely different story. Scotty Bowers in his fascinating book *Full Service* relates that heterosexuals who requested his services rarely asked for more than a redhead or big tits, while homosexuals were extremely demanding. And it's true. That was the problem in Berlin. The beautiful boys were in private clubs and in private hands, wealthy hands, hands that could offer far more than Isherwood's ten marks, even if ten marks were extremely generous for what was available. The boys who went with Isherwood thought he was fabulously rich because they were fabulously lacking in the attributes that would place them in an entirely different class. That said, Isherwood wrote that there were so many postulants that he always found a handsome lad for the night.

Boys of quality in pre-WWI Berlin were in private hands,
not Auden and Isherwood's.

Then, as today, coke was ubiquitous, except that it had just been invented, by Albert Niemann, and was not only fully accepted, it was recommended by Freud to his patients. Klaus Mann preferred heroine but also took cocaine, said to circulate like cigarettes, and everyone was into other drugs, like morphine and opium. After using coke one writer said, ''I felt exhilarated, strong and capable of going on without tiredness.'' Some doctors and researchers believed that men became homosexual when using cocaine, that the drug was the cause, while most believed that coke simply lessened inhibitions, which liberated men with latent homosexuality or bisexuality to free themselves from self-imposed restraints. Cocaine helped one become more sociable and less shy.

Lederhosen provided immediate and all-inclusive access.

In Berlin Auden, Isherwood and their friend Spender spent their time in the Furbinger Strasse, the gay area with its male brothels, and where Auden could count on his favorite boy, Pieps, to beat him up, Auden's preferred form of defilement.

The sudden liberation from fear that followed WWI created a state of euphoria, when men realized that they had survived, which was far from the case for the millions, *millions* whose bodies nurtured the soil of France and Germany, where acre after acre of tombstones are now grassy havens of peace, and whose memorials, with their interminable lists of names, are sentinels at the entrance of every single village and town. The liberation from such a destiny fed an explosion of gaiety, an explosion of relief that life could now resume, and that at the very minimum it had to be seized, cherished and drained, like a perfect liquor, to the last drop.

Such was the catalyst of the roaring 1920s. Such was the boom in expectations that fired the world's most sexually liberated capital, pre-WWII Berlin. The choice of Berlin was no accident, as the roots of sexual emancipation went far deeper, so deep in fact that many historiographers refer to the city as having *invented* homosexuality.

It is said that Auden suffered from two major life failings, the first when he went to Spain to help in its Civil War and was rejected because he hadn't his card to the Communist Party (and certainly, too, because of his milquetoast appearance), and the second when Chester Kallman refused to be faithful to him, a demand that simply does not exist in Sodom where the promise within each new levis crotch is to die for, sight unseen. Kallman, aged 18 to Auden's 32, had apparently thrown himself at Auden during a poetry reading, offering his body--an offer that would continue to the end of Auden's life because they would never leave each other, even if sex soon stopped and Kallman went on sowing his wild oats where he wished.

Kallman and Auden.

Auden never stopped working: poems; film scripts; essays; reviews; more poems, some book length; along with travel--a trip to China with Isherwood--a travel book *Letters from Iceland* with Louis MacNeice; a *mariage blanc* with Erika Mann so she could become a British citizen; and stays in America where he took American citizenship, causing a scandal that reached the floor of parliament. For a while he lived in Brooklyn with Carson McCullers and Benjamin Britten, whose *Billy Bud* is the only opera without a single woman. Summers in Ischia (British gays, again, have historically craved Italian boys--and rightly so) and the first home he ever owned, in Austria. He taught English in Britain and America where he wrote for *The New Yorker* and *The New York Review of Books*. He wrote plays with Isherwood and the libretto for Stravinsky's opera *The Rakes Progress* with Kallman, and one of his poems was read aloud in the film *Four Weddings and a Funeral*. An anthology of all his work would fill thousands of pages. How much remains is for the reader to decide.

Kallman inherited the entirety of Auden's estate and died in Athens at age 54, intestate, his and Auden's heritage going to Kallman's eighty-year-old father.

Auden was said to have been extremely knowledgeable, funny, kind and generous. He once stated that pornography excited him more than a living person, and this was certainly true in his case.

Auden died in 1973 at age 66.

Stephen Spender went to University College, Oxford, where he knew both Isherwood and Auden intimately, and even hand-reprinted Auden's first poems. He was well acquainted with the Bloomsbury Set (4) as well as Berlin at the sides of Auden and Isherwood. He started a novel about the Weimar Republic and the pre-war openness of Germany (meaning easy access to lads), a novel called *The Temple* that he finished in 1988, at age 79 with still 7 years to live.

Spender and one of his boys.

Highly disturbed when Russia joined forces with Germany, Spender wrote an essay about his disillusionment in a book of other essays, *The God that Failed.* He taught in both America and England, poetry and rhetoric. Around age 30 he had homosexual relation with Lucian Freud, a teenager, Sigmund's grandson, although Lucian, an artist, went on to father 14 children he acknowledged and 25 he didn't, while Spender went on to marry twice (having as one of his many lovers Michael Redgrave, Vanessa's father.) Spender's letters to Lucian were put up for sale by his son Matthew Spender, age 70, and went for £35,000.

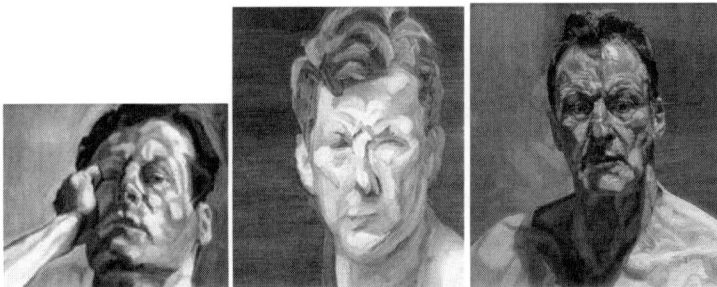

Lucian Freud by himself.

Isherwood had first met Auden at Repton School and as a young man was the lover of the violinist André Mangeot. Isherwood was a tutor in Berlin as in *Cabaret*, the 1972 film version of his book *Goodbye to Berlin.* It was in Berlin that he met the first love of his life, Heinz Neddermeyer, 17, who traveled widely with Isherwood but was imprisoned in Germany for 1½ years for mutual masturbation, plus 2 years of compulsory military service. Heinz later married and had a son, Christian.

Isherwood wrote plays with Auden, one of which was *The Dog Beneath the Skin*, about a man searching for a missing heir, accompanied by a dog that was the heir himself in disguise. Another was *The Ascent of F6,* about a man who accepted an offer by the British press to climb a mountain, F6, ahead of native climbers, but in his haste was killed. Benjamin Britten, with whom Isherwood had lived, wrote the music for the play.

Mangeot on the left.

In California he took in Truman Capote, a boy everyone wanted to have before he destroyed himself physically, for me the best writer who has ever lived. Isherwood produced a book of photographs with texts with photographer and lover Bill Caskey in 1949.

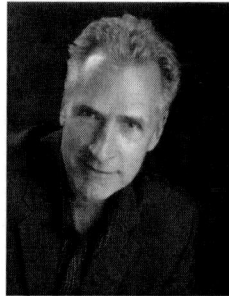

Bill Caskey

The 48-year-old Isherwood met the 18-year-old Don Bachardy on a beach of Santa Monica and spent the rest of his life with the boy, along with the usual ups-and-downs and multiple infidelities on both sides. A film about their lives, *Chris & Don: A Love Story* was released in 2008. Bachardy became an accomplished artist who painted numerous pictures of Isherwood, especially near the end, too sad to be reproduced here. During this time Isherwood taught English at the Los Angeles State College.

Isherwood wrote that he did to his lovers what all lovers do, ''sucking, fucking and rimming''. With that truism in mind we can close the chapter on the foursome, Auden, Isherwood, Spender and Kallman.

PART VII

THE ORIGIN OF PRUSSIAN HOMOSEXUALITY

Before the 1800s men were omnisexual. The Greeks bedded women but preferred men. The Romans were, sexually, largely half and half. Christianity made loving one's male neighbor a sin (except between Catholic clergy and choirboys [tut-tut]) and the same-sex part of omnisexuality largely went underground, with the exception of the Renaissance where it was common for men to seduce boys age 9 or older. Purely homosexual men like de Vinci and Michelangelo were rare; most others, like Cellini, extolled the beauty of boys although Cellini claimed that his best night ever had been with a girl.

In the 1800s Victorian men who preferred only boys gathered in places of male prostitution, the molly houses, in parks and outside barracks, and formed associations like the Bloomsbury Set and the Apostles, although the root of boy love was in the major prep schools and colleges where dormitories were jaded with no-holds-barred orgies, absolute sanctuaries where lads could discover, among themselves, their degree of homosexuality, heterosexuality or bisexuality.

Germany was the hub of homosexuality, with sociological investigations under the likes of Magnus Hirschfeld, and kiosks showed the works of soft-core pornographers like Adolf Brand. France liberated homosexuality in 1791 and the Netherlands soon followed. Prussia was a fertile soil for male-male sex (one could hardly call what went on in Berlin, in hundreds of male whorehouses, *love*), as Germany is today, along with America and what has always been a boy-paradise: Italy--since its founding by the supremely virile lover of boys, the Trojan Aeneus (3). Eternal Italy, the eternal Mecca for homosexual Germans and Brits even before Byron (4), yet the only European country in 2016 that does not allow some form of legal union between boys (even though the source of the blockage, the Catholic church, disburses millions in damages to cover the sodomitical practices of *thousands* of its priests).

It was in the 1800s that homosexuality broke off from omnisexuality to become a distinct version of sexuality, a schism as great as that between Catholics and Protestants. One was classed, definitively, homosexual or heterosexual, bisexuality being a catchall for those who, oftentimes, refused to admit their homosexuality. Yet thanks to Internet the barriers are once again breaking down, and the omnisexuality of Greece and Rome is making a gradual comeback. Those who are mostly homosexual see, on their computer screens, when watching the performances of their favorite male heterosexuals, that a woman's cunt isn't all that harrowing, and those boys who are mainly but not totally heterosexual see the ease of encounters between boys, that boys are just out for pleasure, that they don't need to be wined and dined before being bedded, that they say goodbye without manifestations of jealousy, and that lads give the very best head because they've known since puberty the techniques that turn them on.

Even as far back as the Greeks there were certainly, like today, men who would only go with other men, as there were certainly men who preferred girls, like the boy so ridiculed by his friends for not sharing physical pleasure with them that he prayed to Zeus to allow him, too, to appreciate love between boys. When this didn't happen, he killed himself.

Appearances can be deceiving. In the Florence of Lorenzo de' Medici a man could be burned for homosexuality, yet in reality one had to rape a child in order to go up in smoke. Sex with boys was otherwise so common (da Vinci was arrested three times for partaking in boy-charms), practiced by so many--and especially by so many nobles--that the men got off with a fine, which enriched the officials who collected it (10). Laws in France after the Revolution, enacted in 1791 under the renowned homosexual Cambacérès, *de*criminalized sodomy, although there were laws against indecency, laws that any official could use to imprison anyone they wished. (Those same laws saw my personal arrest and interrogation at the famous Quai des Orfèvres, after a club I frequented was raided and the boys hauled away because during a slow dance they were entwined, deemed indecent at that time.) In Germany too the anti-sodomy statute of 1871 (Paragraph 175) could have had a damaging effect had it been applied with vigor, which was not the case.

In 1813 Bavaria allowed same-sex unions, except concerning boys under age 12, and rape was severely punished. Baden and Württemberg followed suit in 1815, but all three had laws defending public decency. During this time homosexuality was still punished in Prussia, Austria, Saxony, Hamburg and Bremen.

Germany is called the homeland of homosexuality because where the French, the Italians and the British decided to let sleeping dogs lie, the Germans rose up against statutes forbidding certain forms of sexuality, investing huge amounts of time in newspaper articles and conferences and magazines and organizations, like Hirschfeld's, to have them overturned. Luckily the press had been freed by Frederick the Great, who had allowed even Voltaire to publish the list of his male lovers, as reported.

Isherwood liked the club called the Cozy Corner where young laborers waited for clients while playing cards, their shirts open to the belt and sleeves rolled up over their muscular biceps. These boys often came from unhappy families, usually accompanied by extreme poverty. The Karlsbad Café sold drugs and gigolos sold themselves. Isherwood and Klaus Mann liked workers, Mann noting in his journal that he went to the Parisian, in

1933, where he was presented to a sailor he didn't care for, so moved on to the Jockey were he "made out" with a certain Freddy, followed by a "young peasant with an enormous thing" he picked up in the street. A few weeks later he went to the baths where the masseur "didn't dare try anything" and the clients were too fat. A month afterwards he had a threesome. Later still he went to the Private Club where there were "a lot of transvestites", and ended the night with "Willy". Other well-known transvestite bars and clubs were the Eldorado, the Mikado, the Silhouette. The Amicitia was a favored café, and the Palast-Europe, Palast-Papagei, Marien-Kasino, Windsbona-Kasino and Kleist-Kasino were popular watering holes for boys seeking boys.

Mug shots of prostitute and cross-dresser Johann Scheff. Although there were certainly magnificent boys to be had, lederhosen deeply-tanned athletes, Scheff was most probably the run-of-the-mill variety for daily consumption.

Soldiers and sailors could be given a rapid blowjob for 50 pfennig, while the best boys went for 80 marks, although 5 seemed to have been the average amount. The elite could earn 400 marks a month, but they circulated among the rich and only wound up in clubs as they aged, and then on the street in their mid or late twenties. Many boys just wanted a meal and a bed for the night, in which case how many johns saw the dawn without being beaten up or, at the minimum, robbed, is unknown. The safest way was to get a boy by means of a hotel porter who, naturally, received part of the payments, and Florence Tamagne, in her excellent *A History of Homosexuality in Europe*, 2004, states that a number of boys liked to latch on to foreigners and tour Europe with them, passing themselves off as the "nephews" of their "uncles", (which reminds me of a brief period in Paris where I too had been a "nephew").

Handsome, well-turned boys could perhaps amass enough to open a tobacco shop or café or bar, but their working life was short, ending normally in their early twenties, lives they could have begun as schoolboys, perhaps 17, although age 14 was far from exceptional. Hamburg was also a gay site, especially around Sankt Pauli, popular in the 1930s and still going strong 60 years later, when I discovered it, although the estimated 3,000 male-rent in the '30s had *seemingly* evaporated in the '90s. But then, the unemployment of the '30s had nothing to do with the full employment after the '50s.

Sex was an enormous leveler between the classes, when famous writers and eminent professors settled down with working-class chaps, both entirely satisfied. The idea that boys-will-be-boys has freed lads to do as they wish even when still dwelling in caves. Male-rent was never as ill-considered as female prostitution, and many upper-class men dropped into the working classes to find boys they had a truly loving relationship with, relationships men did not often have with women. The boys may have started out as rent, but love or a form of love won out, and both at times ended up in adjoining graves. (I'm thinking of George Merrill and Edward Carpenter's graves, and of John Finch and Thomas Baines' chapel [9].) Men like Isherwood would proudly display their boys, with there never being the slightest hint to inequality between them. And if the boy left, the man would often suffer--and vice versa. A man with a handsome lad was envied in a way that didn't exist with female hookers with whom one rarely spent more than a night. And the boys could become famous, with their own biographers, like Tennessee's Frank Merlo who answered, when asked what he did for a living: I sleep with Mr. Williams.

Freud

Freud believed that all men were latently bisexual, and that from this latency some men took an exclusively homosexual route, others omnisexuality, still others part-time homosexuality, and a category that was situational-homosexual when in a boarding-school context or in the army or in prison or spending the night with a friend when it ''just happened'' or giving mutual helping-hand relief as during the Princeton rub.

A childhood fixation with the mother, loving what she loved, which was men, was considered a prime cause, the reason why homosexuality was so natural in Ionian Greece and Dorian Sparta where boys were placed with women until the age of 7, but also in England where boys were cared for by wet nurses and nannies before entering boarding schools where sex between boys was a daily occurrence. Thackeray, on his first day of school, was hailed by a lad who invited him to come and frig him, while J.A. Symonds reveals nightly orgies of disgusting raunchiness (according to the often sanctimonious Symonds, but perhaps not all that disgusting to the participants). Many of these boys did become exclusively homosexual later in life, many others bisexual, although the vast majority married and founded families, perhaps for societal reasons, perhaps like Thomas Mann to ensure his financial well-being, or perhaps because they were basically heterosexual (in my book *Boarding School Homosexuality* I relate the story of one lad who had had every boy in his school, but once he left school he had every girl who came his way too).

A father can add to his son's homosexuality by being absent, perhaps through work, perhaps because he died when the boy was young, which is the case for a huge number of German boys whose fathers were killed during the wars there. Or perhaps the boy just didn't get on well with his dad, hated him even, many of whom revolted (and then turned to crime, the reason why sex is so prevalent between men in prisons, theorize some researchers), while other boys sublimated their homosexuality into art, like Michelangelo who despised his father, his father who stated than none of his sons would give him so much as a drink of water if he were dying of thirst. Freud wrote that thanks to sublimation a man could carry on in a heterosexual manner, and he rejected the idea that one could be born with his sexual orientation already determined. A homosexual father often turns out homosexual sons, as Thomas Mann's Golo and Klaus (whose lives are related later), while Mann's son Michael was bisexual.

It is true that sex is easy between boys because they are identical. Boys in Naples claimed, during a televised interview, that they had first sex with transsexuals because they knew their bodies and knew what to expect. And because boys often discover first sex together, the ease could last throughout a lifetime. When boarding-school lads had their first experiences with girls, many were put off by the incredible anatomical differences.

Freud felt that confirmed homosexuals could not be changed because they in no way suffered from their being gay (like Tim Cooke of Apple who even thanked God for his gift of homosexual orientation). People who want to change their sexuality for societal reasons (like the insults he hears daily in a looker-room situation) can never change their orientation, and indeed, Freud would accept them for analysis only if they were suffering neurotically from being homosexual, in which case he would accept them as patients but only to help them accept themselves as being homosexual.

At any rate, Freud said that the whys and wherefores of homosexuality remained the greatest mystery of his life, which the vagueness of this chapter fully demonstrates.

William (Wilhelm) Reich (1897 – 1957), worked closely with Freud. His name was yelled out by students during the May '68 Student Revolt in Paris because he encouraged coeducation, with the sexes allowed to mingle and have intercourse when they desired to do so. His life defies belief, and concerns us because he was born in Austria-Hungary (now the Ukraine) and had extremely liberal views concerning homosexuality. In his diaries he told of trying to have sex with the family maid with whom he slept in the same bed, at age 4, and at age 11 he was fucking the family servants daily. He started visiting brothels at age 15 and daily at age 17. When he found out his mother was sleeping with one of his tutors he threatened to reveal all to his father if she didn't allow him to fuck her. She refused, he did as he threatened to do, and she killed herself (he was 13).

At age 3, a year before....

Reich fought in WWI and at age 22, while studying medicine, he met Freud who was so impressed by him that he gave Reich patients to analyze. Reich was accused of making his first patient pregnant and then of killing her in a botched abortion attempt. The girl's mother protested to the authorities and Reich claimed she did so because he had refused her sexual advances. She too committed suicide. Reich's biographer, Myron Sharaf, claimed Reich ordered other women and even his wives to have abortions, perhaps to spare him the cost of raising the children.

Reich around age 25.

74

He became a medical doctor and then studied neuropsychiatry under Nobel Prize Winner in Medicine Julius Wagner von Jauregg. He became an assistant director of Freud's Vienna clinic in 1924 at age 27. He gave seminars and his eloquence was described as enchanting and spellbinding. His presence and domination over others was, he himself wrote, "like a shark in a pond of carps."

He wrote erudite books extremely well received, especially by his mentor Freud. He championed "orgasmic potency", stating that psychic health depended on the full discharge of the libido, that was "not just fucking but included all of the excitation leading up to fucking" (his words). "The more intense the preliminaries, the more intense is the orgasm, and the more satisfying and fulfilling the release." In this he seems to have been criticized, labeled the "prophet of a better organism", the "founder of genital utopia" and the man who believed that an orgasm was the solution to every neurosis.

He opened a number of clinics that gave free medical advice in contraception as well as psychoanalytic counseling, and he joined the Communist Party. His clinic became mobile. He drove into the suburbs and parks with a team of psychoanalysts and doctors, with advice, counsel and contraceptives. Even children were included in his effort at enlightenment, and teenagers encouraged to fully explore their sexuality. His promotion of teenage sex eventually got him excluded by the Danish Communist Party (Denmark, today, considered the world's happiest country, perhaps because it has [knowingly or not knowingly] incorporated certain of Reich's liberating concepts).

Reich had experiments using students in which they kissed and touched while Reich measured their body reactions on an oscillograph. One such student was the future chancellor Willy Brandt. Reich and his son spent a great deal of time looking for UFOs and in America he invented the orgone accumulator in which the buyer--for example Norman Mahler (who owned several), Ginsberg, J.D. Salinger, Jack Kerouac and many others-- sat naked and were cured of cancer.

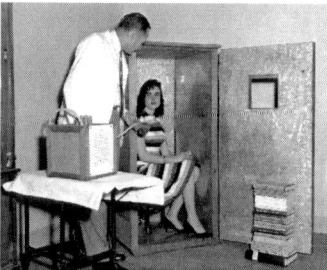

His Orgone Accumulator. His museum in Orgonon Maine

Imprisoned for being a charlatan, Reich was found dead in his cell, apparently of a heart attack.

Freud and his thoughts on homosexuality are perplexing. On the one hand his belief that we all start out as bisexuals, that homosexuality is too rooted in a man to be altered, and that homosexuals are every bit as virile as heterosexuals, seems sound. Whereas, on the other hand, he was deeply interested in Eugen Steinach's attempt to replace a homosexual's testicles with those of a heterosexual, which is strange to say the least.

In fact, Freud's clearest view on the subject was in response to a letter from a woman who feared for her son: ''I gather from your letter that your son is a homosexual. I am most impressed by the fact that you do not mention this term yourself in your information about him. May I question you why you avoid it? Homosexuality is assuredly no advantage, but it is nothing to be ashamed of, no vice, no degradation; it cannot be classified as an illness; we consider it to be a variation of the sexual function. Many highly respectable individuals of ancient and modern times have been homosexuals, several of the greatest men among them. (Plato, Michelangelo, Leonardo da Vinci, etc). It is a great injustice to persecute homosexuality as a crime--and a cruelty, too.

''What analysis can do for your son runs in a different line. If he is unhappy, neurotic, torn by conflicts, inhibited in his social life, analysis may bring him harmony, peace of mind, full efficiency, whether he remains homosexual or not.''

The complexity of why a boy becomes homosexual is such that psychiatrists seem to throw up their hands, ceding their places to those scientists in search of a ''gay gene'' that will miraculously explain it all. In the lack of such a discovery it's easy to give credence to those who think that homosexuality is largely based on Narcissism: self-love that leads one to choose an object that resembles himself, a concept easy to understand, but in that case, in today's ''me'' world, shouldn't there be far more homosexuals than there are, because what boy isn't in love with himself? What boy doesn't kiss his reflection in the mirror? What boy hasn't gotten hard admiring the beauty of his own body?

PRUSSIAN DEFENDERS OF HOMOSEXUALITY

The most tolerant gay-friendly nation in the world is, of course, America, San Francisco its Holy Land, but Berlin comes in a clear second today, a capital that celebrates the gay-way every June in a march called Christopher Street Day in remembrance of the Stonewall Revolt, as I reported in the Introduction.

Throughout history, excluding the hellish interval of the Nazi maelstrom, Prussia has been tolerant of homosexuals, the word itself invented in 1869 by Karl-Maria Kertbeny and publically defended for the first time in 1867 by the jurist Karl Heinrich Ulrichs in Munich. In 1897 Magnus Hirschfeld founded the first organization in the defense of homosexuality, the Scientific Humanitarian Committee.

Naturally, all of this is hardly a hill of beans in comparison to the hallowed age of our distant ancestors, the Greeks, but in our times of rabid dissent, with nearly daily beheadings, the Age of Pericles is certainly lost to us forever: A crucifixion supposed to free men brought instead a veil of lead that has extinguished the light and closed off the minds of Western man for over 2,000 years.

Karl Ulrichs quoted Schopenhauer from his *The World as Will and Representation* in which he wrote that homosexuality was in every culture: ''It arises in some way from human nature itself.'' Schopenhauer was in no way infallible because he added: ''It occurred in the old as Nature's way of keeping a man from procreating.'' Ulrichs went on to note, *à propos* of nothing at all, that homosexuals were drawn to Wagner's magnificent, if syrupy operas, the proof being the popularity to our own day of the Festival of Bayreuth with its well-heeled and well-dressed gays.

In 1885 the Berlin police commissioner Leopold von Meerscheidt-Hüllessem founded the Department of Homosexuals to keep track of them for the seemingly benevolent reason of freeing homosexuals from blackmail and the resultant suicides. He personally conducted tours for the rich through the gay dives of the city, where he knew the boys by name, tours that perhaps brought him money from those who were out to do a little slumming because he eventually killed himself when caught accepting bribes from a banker he was protecting from accusations of rape.

It was largely thanks to Meerscheidt-Hüllessem's *laissez-faire* attitude that homosexual restaurants, clubs, bars, indoor and outdoor dance halls and costume balls flourished, and homosexual playgrounds alongside rivers, lakes, canals and railways became popular for immediate consumption. Sexual liberation in Berlin was a drawing power, but equally so was the fact that there was something for everyone: cross-dressers, their cheeks rouged and their eyebrows plucked; sadists paid to stomp on the likes of masochistic Auden; virile hustlers who let johns feel their yards through their trousers, often of military fabrication as soldiers and sailors were well aware of the appeal of their uniforms and positioned themselves just outside their barracks or along the Unter den Linden, in the Tiergarten Park and Friedrichstrasse, known for its prostitutes, and Berlin's Broadway, the Ku' damm. The more one aged, the more one was obliged to exchange the warmth and ambience of clubs and bars in search of johns outside, in parks and along streets, in bath houses and swimming pools.

Magnus Hirschfeld was ostracized by most homosexuals because of his interest in effeminacy, lesbians and cross-dressers, all of which undermined a homosexual man's image of himself as being more virile than straights because homosexuals changed partners more often and had sex more often. This was largely true because men were out for an orgasm, preferably in parks, forests and the like (outdoor sex was always an added stimulant), unions that could rapidly increase in the number of participants out for the same thrill. There was no convincing as was a necessity with women, although heterosexuals maintained that such rites boosted one's lust, while homosexuals knew that what really excited were a few minutes with an unknown male, discovering the mysterious contents shielded by the buttons of a pair of trousers, in places as dangerously exposed as possible.

Karl August Georg Maximilian Graf von Platen-Hallermünde

Karl August Georg Maximilian Graf von Platen-Hallermünde (1796 – 1835) was admitted to the royal school of pages at age 14. He served as a lieutenant in France and studied philosophy and philology at the University of Würzburg. He wrote several volumes of homoerotic poems and took up residence in Italy, especially Florence, Rome and Naples where he could give full vent to his homosexuality among the world's most beautiful lads. He went to Sicily where he moved from place to place in fear of cholera that was decimating the island, but the epidemic caught up with him at age 39 in Syracuse.

Von Platen

Karl-Maria Kertbeny

It was Karl-Maria Kertbeny (1824 – 1882) who coined the words homosexual and heterosexual (and monosexuality for masturbators). He translated the works of Musset, Hans Christian Anderson and the Grimm Brothers into German. The author of 25 books, many on travel, he was drawn to the defense of homosexuals when a gay friend killed himself when blackmailed. Himself heterosexual, he simply believed that people should have the right to do as they wished in the privacy of their bedrooms.

His importance to my eyes was his assertion that homosexuality was inborn and unchangeable, and that homosexuals were not effeminate, the opposite of what Ulrichs and Hirschfeld preached.

His gravesite in Prague was searched out and refurbished by local gays in 2002, and adorned with wreaths since then.

Karl Heinrich Ulrichs

Karl Heinrich Ulrichs (1825 – 1895) was the founder of a gay rights movement. Introduced to male-male sex by his riding instructor at age 14, he graduated from Berlin University with a diploma in history and a dissertation in Latin. He wrote *Studies on the Riddle of Male-Male Love* (also translated as *Man-Manly Love*), giving the names of Uranian to gays, a designation that happily didn't stick, nor did his assertion that homosexuals possessed a female psyche in a male body. Instead of being repulsed by some of Ulrichs' declarations, his followers were grateful because now they knew they were not alone, that there were others who shared their passion, although many refused to believe that homosexual men were largely women trapped in a male shell.

Ulrichs was so well known and respected that one of his supporters, disappointed when Ulrichs declared, ''a homosexual had the heart of a woman in the body of a man'', acknowledged it must be true as Ulrichs was a specialist. The supporter was nonetheless glad when Ulrichs stated that homosexuality was not an illness but a variation of sexuality like the varying color of one's hair or eyes.

Goldsworthy Lowes Dickinson, a diplomat, wrote that he too was surprised to learn that he had a feminine soul in a male body, but he apparently believed Ulrichs. Dickinson, an Englishman, initiated the idea of the League of Nations. Called Goldie, he entered the boarding school of Beomonds, then Charterhouse School, from ages 14 to 19, followed by King's College, Cambridge. In 1896 he wrote *The Greek View of Life*. Forster wrote the biography of Dickinson after Dickinson's death in 1932 but omitted all information concerning Dickinson's homosexuality and foot fetishism. Dickinson had been involved in both the Apostles and the Bloomsbury Set (9). He wrote dozens of books, one of which was *The Magic Flute: A Fantasia to Plato and his Dialogues*.

Ulrichs' relationships with young men were both sexual and fatherly, certainly an ideal figure for a boy needing warm guidance from a man who would show him the way, instructing him intellectually while satisfying him tenderly and perhaps physically, yet without the virile dimension so vital in Ancient Greece. His notion that men where mere male shells inhabited by a woman's urges and psyche was nonetheless adopted by a disconcerting number of psychiatrists and neurologists, one of whom was Richard von Krafft-Ebing who added to Ulrichs' ideas by stating that homosexuals suffered from deformations and disorders, and could therefore not be punished under Paragraph 175 for what nature imposed on them.

Ulrichs was the first man to publicly defend homosexuality, in the Congress of German Jurists in Munich in 1867. His books were banned throughout Prussia, although the writings that survived were republished in 2004.

After Ulrichs' death Friedländer (whose story is coming up) wrote that Ulrichs ''had been a true pioneer, and only now, a generation later, is homosexuality no longer un-discussable,'' underlining how Ulrichs had been shouted down when he first stood in the Congress of German Jurists and begged the delegates to at least consider homosexual rights.

Ulrichs crossed the Alps in 1880, on foot, joining other Prussian and British homosexuals who regularly made the pilgrimage, thanks to Italy's sexual freedom and lusty, beautiful lads, a pilgrimage that took him to Florence, Ravenna, Naples, Rome and elsewhere. He received a diploma from the University of Naples and died in L'Aquila, a devotee to Italian boys to his last breath. Like the pilgrimages to the temple of Iolaus in Ancient Greece, lads today visit his tomb, refurbished by the locals in thanks for gay visitors' financial largess, and I'm sure the local boys turn out to profit from gay wealth too, a gold coin that has been the alchemy, from the Romans, known to stiffen a boy's hidden treasures.

Richard von Krafft-Ebing
The Masturbation Panic

Richard von Krafft-Ebing (1840 – 1902) was an extremely influent Austrian psychiatrist, a medico-legal authority on sexual pathology, whose book *Psychopathia Sexualis* contained 238 case histories of human sexual behavior, that Freud (happily) relegated to the dustbin of history.

The purpose of sexual desire, wrote Krafft-Ebing, was exclusively procreation, ''and every other form of sex must be regarded as perverse.'' Homosexual libido was a moral vice whose origin was early masturbation. He angered the Catholic church by writing that martyrdom was a form of hysteria and masochism, a judgment the reader is free to assess for himself.

Masturbation was held by many as the key to homosexuality, while some researchers claimed--after having examined many men--that active homosexuals had arrow-shaped penises, while their passive counterparts had anuses in the shape of accommodating funnels. Still other physicians found homosexuals to possess small dicks, the reason they were spurned by women who sought out greater sexual satisfaction, and therefore left small-dick guys among themselves: forcing them into homosexuality.

The cause of homosexuality was often attributed to masturbation, but from the 1700s to the 1900s there was even a masturbation panic, caused by the beliefs of certain doctors, most notably a doctor whose name has come down to us, Simon-André Tissot, who claimed that the loss of an ounce of semen equaled the loss of forty ounces of blood, a crippling factor that could lead to the loss of eyesight, to diseases and, due to increased blood flow to the brain, insanity, consequences far more severe than religious repercussions due to the nefarious, unnatural act of self-pleasuring, the mortal enemy of procreation. In the mid-1850s it was blamed for the corruption of morals, as well as vile thoughts that threatened the salvation of the soul itself, accompanied by the exhaustion of the entire nervous system. Boys were ordered to do physical exercises until they dropped from fatigue, to take cold showers, and fathers were advised to tie up their hands at night (presumably behind their backs, although the most exquisite sensation could then be enjoyed by gently rubbing oneself against one's mattress, as the reader well knows). Some surgeons recommended replacing the testicles of masturbators with healthy ones (which could lead to castration because the new testicles were rejected by the body, and death if the surgery was done in unclean surroundings, often the case in those times).

In 1925 Adolf Brand wrote that prudent masturbation ''absolutely cannot be harmful. What is worse is to forbid sexual self-satisfaction to young people. A prohibition cannot be kept, since the sexual drive in young people absolutely requires satisfaction. And since the forbidden fruit is doubly enticing, it contributes to the attainment of sexual self-satisfaction. Only under secrecy can self-satisfaction, which is natural and healthy, become a sexual vice.''

Intercourse too was to be restricted to procreation, because if it were practiced too often the result would be the same as for masturbation, the proof being the loss of energy and extreme fatigue after spilling one's seed. This was reinforced by the fact that men in asylums openly masturbated. The final choice was between going to Hell or ending up insane, little wonder the period was known for its masturbation panic. Today things have changed to the extent that a lad is considered a prude if he refrains from jerking off in the presence of a college roommate, as well as lots of other damning things open to the brave of heart.

Magnus Hirschfeld

Magnus Hirschfeld (1868 – 1935) was a sexologist who practiced in Berlin. He founded the Scientific Humanitarian Committee with others in 1897, the two-fold interest of which was 1) to abrogate the 1871 law criminalizing homosexuality and 2) to try to convince people that thanks to scientific understanding hostility to homosexuals would eventually be eliminated.

Hirschfeld's work was inspired by a military officer who committed suicide on the eve of his wedding, preferring death to what would be required on his honeymoon night, an epiphany for Hirschfeld, Beachy relates.

Alas, he believed that homosexuality was a debility (†) and that homosexuals were effeminate, thus provoking a schism in his group and the formation of a second society, founded by those who believed that male-male love was another form of virile manliness. († Light-years from Tim Cooke, President of Apple, who said: "I consider being gay among the greatest gifts God has given me.")

Hirschfeld introduced a bill for the abrogation of the 1871 law (Paragraph 175), reinforced by a petition of 5,000 names, among them Hermann Hesse, Stefan Zweig, Thomas Mann, Zola, Tolstoy, Rainer Maria Rilke, Herman Hesse and Einstein (Alfred Krupp refused to sign). When the bill didn't pass, Hirschfeld turned to outing the legislators who had voted against it, a tool used for the very first time. Hirschfeld then envisaged a massive outing of the members of his own societies, which would tie up the courts until the abrogation of Paragraph 175, but because so many men, like the millionaire Krupp, chose suicide over outing, that path was abandoned due to the mountain of corpses it would entail. The bill did make some progress in the 1920s but came to a screeching halt with Hitler.

There then came the Harden-Eulenburg interlude in Hirschfeld's life: Harden was a journalist who wrote that General Kuno von Moltke was having a homosexual affair with Prince Philip von Eulenburg. Hirschfeld, as an expert on homosexuality, testified in Harden's favor, stating that Moltke was indeed homosexual (thanks to "waves" homosexuals emitted, that Hirschfeld had been trained to detect). In doing so Hirschfeld hoped that once people knew that someone as virile as a general could be gay, they would decide to make homosexuality legal. The jury found Harden innocent of libel in 1907 but the judge, enraged with homosexuals who had "the morals of dogs", overturned the decision. A new trial was ordered and Harden was found guilty and sent to prison for four months. Further backlash came when anti-Semites, who hated the Jew Hirschfeld, defended the Aryan Eulenburg. In the end, Hirschfeld decided he had caused more trouble in outing Moltke than good for the homosexual cause. (The full story to follow.)

Dubbed the Einstein of sex, Hirschfeld opened the Institute for Sexual Research in the liberal Weimar Republic in 1919, that housed a Museum of Sex and had some 50 rooms, one of which was occupied for a time by Christopher Isherwood and visited by W.H. Auden, André Gide and Sergei Eisenstein. There was a museum with sex toys and walls plastered with photos of nudes, presumably there for sexual education, and lots of men dressed as women and women as men, both in photos and live as visitors. Teas were offered at the Institute, reigned over by Hirschfeld and his lover Karl Giese. Bar hopping at night was included, so that in one way or another one could meet and mate with whomever one wished, back ''home'' at the Institute. For those passing through like Isherwood the occasions to meet boys, the private rooms and stacks of pornography, made the Institute a lad's wet dream.

Giese sitting next to Hirschfeld, on the left of the picture.

The Institute was manned by doctors, interns and students working on their PhDs, and gave sexual instruction on birth control, venereal diseases and offered hormonal treatments and the first tries at transsexual surgery. In one operation a man who wanted to become a woman had his penis sort of pushed inside-out into a cavity, but when he later fell in love with a woman the surgery was reversed, with supposedly satisfying results; the patient, at any rate, went on to become a pathologist, recounts Beachy. Hirschfeld established 64 degrees of sexuality, from masculine heterosexual males to feminine homosexual males, with transsexuals somewhere along the line.

There was never-ending, at times extremely catty, philosophical, medical and scientific disagreements between all the men involved in the sexual research, especially those who foamed at the mouth when Hirschfeld called them an effeminate third sex. Relations were therefore far from a long, calm river, with, indeed, some furious rapids, especially when some men stole the boyfriends of other researchers. The police occasionally got in the way, finding some Institute-friendly publications immoral, such as *Der Eigene* that was once fined 5,000 marks.

The more Hirschfeld gained in renown the more he inspired jealously, especially from those who vomited his emphasis on homosexuals being a third girly-like sex, as well as the attention he paid to cross-dressers and androgynes (those who are not entirely men or women). His enemies considered themselves equal to all other virile males, equal to the Ancient Greeks and their relations centered on men's love for boys. Hirschfeld's embryonic bisexuality favored heterosexuals due to Darwin's law that whatever favored heterosexuality flourished because heterosexuals procreated while homosexuals didn't, except under societal pressures as found in Victorian England where men more or less had to marry, and in the States today where men like politicians haven't a snowball's chance in Hell of survival if they are outed, and the best way to not be outed is to reproduce.

Hirschfeld did great harm in stating that homosexuals as children were recognizable because they preferred cooking, playing with dolls and mixing with girls; they sought to please, choosing intellectual, emotive and artistic values over manual labor and solid reasoning. This hit home with me by an incident that happened when I joined the Peace Corps, an incident I would like to relate here as proof of what homosexuals had to go through a very few years ago (and still undergo, but in a much more insidious fashion): Home for me was a room with three beds and two cots. It was my first experience at sharing, and I disliked it. The guys made noise until all hours, they monopolized the bathroom and they looked on me with scorn because I wouldn't take part in their pastimes: I refused to shuffle-and-giggle-and-ah-shucks-should-we? on the doorsteps of strip joints; I despised their music, their idiotic jokes and their pigskin heroes. The underlying abyss was, as always, sex. Without that common denominator we were invariably at odds. The boys farted openly, they belched like Turks, one used the can while a second pissed in the sink and a third combed his hair looking over his shoulder. Mark was as manly as any of them, and except for whom he screwed, Mark's interests were mine. We both liked music and our favorite topic was books, and we were both keen on sports: Mark competitive ones, me those made for loners, like swimming and athletics. Yet when the volunteers had their three-day battery of psychological tests, Mark came out an A-1 male while I had to go through an unexpected interview with a bulbous-nosed, toady-skinned shrink.

"Uh, the results show you like paintings, sculpture and arty things like that..." I had marked the No Interest box on any question in the least compromising; the corrector had drawn the right conclusions anyway. "Uh, you're a loner ... you know, the type that'd rather sit in the house all day sewing than toss a ball about. Now, Jamaica's a very masculine society and we're not sure if your skills (?) would go over well there..."

I jumped up and sputtered so violently I showered the shrink with spittle: ''I'm no goddamned queer if that's what you're getting at, and if a guy can't like a picture you might as well shut down the goddamned museums....'' The shrink stopped me with a wave of the hand and a supercilious grin and said, "Uh, that's not what I was getting at...." and changed the subject. During the mid-training deselection--based nearly solely on the shrink's report--I was left unscathed. Charlie went though. I cringed at the thought of his limp-wrist rebuttal to the same accusations. When Charlie got the word that he was no longer one of the volunteers, his jowls sagged further still, he went white, and meekly protested, "Well, why *me*?" while giving us all a look of abysmal distress. Sophie came up to help him leave the room before he broke down. He pointed a hip towards the door and followed it out. I wondered if Charlie's sacrifice--statistically there had to be at least *one* among us--had saved me. But I couldn't help wondering how the tests had shown me up and not Mark. Mark who had at least as much "sensitivity" as I, and more "arty" knowledge in his little finger, I knew, than would probably accumulate in me during my entire life. Coming as it did at the beginning of the 80s, such gay phobia didn't seem particularly unjust or even out of place to me. That I had to go through it was just too bad, *just too doggoned bad.* (12)

It didn't even occur to me, until years later, that the injustice of what took place was anything more than simply *too doggoned bad.*

Different From The Others (Anders als die Andern)

That the homosexual film *Different From The Others (Anders als die Andern)* was written by Hirschfeld (and Richard Oswald) and released in 1919 seems incredible. It was a plea for the suppression of Paragraph 175. The film was destroyed by the Nazis in 1933 and the one remaining copy was shown at the 2016 Berlin International Film Festival. The résumé of the film as presented by Wikipedia is so perfect that I'm going to reproduce it as it appears:

The German homosexual actor Conrad Veidt portrays a successful violinist, Paul Körner, who falls in love with one of his male students. A sleazy extortionist threatens to expose Körner as a homosexual. Flashbacks show us how Körner became aware of his orientation and tried first to change it, then to understand it. Körner and the extortionist end up in court, where the judge is sympathetic to the violinist, but when the scandal becomes public, Körner's career is ruined and he is driven to suicide.

The film opens with Paul Körner (Conrad Veidt) reading the daily newspaper obituaries, which are filled with vaguely worded and seemingly inexplicable suicides. Körner, however, knows that Paragraph 175 is hidden behind them all--that it hangs over German homosexuals "like the Sword of Damocles."

Kurt Sivers (actor Fritz Schulz) is a fan and admirer of Körner, a violin virtuoso, and he approaches Körner in hopes of becoming a student of his. Körner agrees and they begin lessons together, during which they fall in love.

Both men experience the disapproval of their parents. Neither are out, but Sivers's parents object to the increasingly large amount of attention he focuses on the violin and his unusual infatuation with Körner, and the Körners do not understand why he has shown no interest in finding a wife and starting a family. Körner sends his parents to see his mentor, the Doctor (Dr. Magnus Hirschfeld).

The Doctor appears several times in the film, each time to deliver speeches more intended for the audience than the advancement of the plot. In this, his first appearance, he tells Körner's parents:

You must not condemn your son because he is a homosexual, he is not to blame for his orientation. It is not wrong, nor should it be a crime. Indeed, it is not even an illness, merely a variation, and one that is common to all of nature.

After Körner's coming out, he and Sivers begin seeing each other more openly. While walking together, hand in hand, through the park, they pass a man who recognizes Körner. Later that day, when Körner is alone, this man, Franz Bollek (actor Reinhold Schünzel) confronts him and demands hush money or else he will expose Sivers.

Körner pays him and keeps it a secret from Sivers that he does so. Eventually, however, the blackmailer's demands become so great that Körner refuses to pay. Bollek decides instead to break into Körner's house while he and Sivers are performing, but he is discovered by Sivers and Körner on their return and a fight breaks out. In the course of the fight, Bollek reveals to Sivers that he has been blackmailing him.

Sivers runs away and faces hardships trying to survive alone. Körner is left dejected and, over a photo of Sivers, remembers his past.

His first memory is of boarding school, when he and his boyfriend Max are discovered kissing by their teacher and he is expelled. Next, he remembers University and his solitary and lonely life there, and the growing impossibility of trying to play straight.

Körner then meets with the doctor, who tells him:

Love for one of the same sex is no less pure or noble than for one of the opposite. This orientation can be found in all levels of society, and among respected people. Those that say otherwise come only from ignorance and bigotry.

Remembering further, he recalled first meeting Bollek at a gay dance hall, and Bollek leading him on before ultimately turning on him and using his homosexuality to blackmail him.

Körner reports Bollek for blackmail and has him arrested. In retaliation, Bollek exposes Körner. The Doctor gives testimony on Körner's behalf, but both are found guilty of their respective crimes. Bollek is sentenced to three years for extortion. The judge is sympathetic to Körner, and gives him the minimum sentence allowable: one week.

Allowed to go home before starting his term, Körner finds himself shunned by friends and strangers alike, and no longer employable. Even his family tells him there is only one honorable way out. He then takes a handful of pills, committing suicide.

Sivers rushes to his side as he lies dead. Körner's parents blame Sivers for what has happened. Sivers attempts to kill himself as well, but the Doctor prevents him and delivers his final speech:

You have to keep living; live to change the prejudices by which this man has been made one of the countless victims. ... (Y)ou must restore the honor of this man and bring justice to him, and all those who came before him, and all those to come after him. Justice through knowledge!

The film closes with an open German law book, turned to Paragraph 175, as a hand holding a brush crosses it out.

Hirschfeld's interventions must have been of immense importance then, and are certainly as much so today.

Friedrich Alfred Krupp

Friedrich Alfred Krupp (1854 – 1902), called Fritz, was born in Essen, home of the Krupp family fortune that he inherited in 1887 at age 33. He was an intimate of the homosexual Emperor Wilhelm II (also known as William II) who defended Krupp's heterosexuality, calling those who applauded his death "men unworthy of the name German." Wilhelm is said to have had Krupp's wife committed to an asylum when she went to him about her husband's preference for boys, perhaps to muzzle his personal involvement with Krupp and Krupp's lads. Like Tiberius before him, Krupp discovered the paradise that is Capri, a rocky island of beautiful flowers, superb climate, virile fishermen and their sons. The homosexuals that made the island their home were soon so numerous that they were obliged to import boys from outside in order to meet their needs, thereby forcing the locals to expulse them for unfair competition, as they did the French writer Jacques d'Adelswärd-Fersen (4).

Krupp himself was ordered out in 1901 when the scandal of his orgies became public knowledge, thanks to a smear campaign organized by the political party SPD in the magazine *Vorwäts*. Krupp's Capri orgies centered around the *Grotta di Frà Felice,* the grounds to which were entered by the lads given golden keys to the gate, and the best performers were said to have been awarded gold pins in the shape of artillery shells. Sex in the grotto was accompanied by a live string quartet and orgasms were celebrated by fireworks (which sounds incredible, yet the reader knowns that nothing of a sexual nature is ever too outlandish, not even Gilles de Rais who may have put up to 100,000 children to death to satisfy his sexual lust, and whose blood was needed for his experiments in alchemy). Krupp's boy participants were often underage, but this was nothing new in that both da Vinci and Cellini's favorites were age 10, and during the Renaissance boys could be had from age 9.

Perhaps fearing a scandal *à la* Oscar Wilde, Krupp committed suicide at age 48. We don't know how because his death was disguised as a heart attack.

Hermann von Teschenberg

Hermann von Teschenberg (1866 – 1911) was a member of Hirschfeld's clique, the cross-dressing son of a diplomat who had fled his native Vienna when caught kissing a soldier in a park. He married but finished his life in Naples, an extremely favored site for German homosexuals. He translated some of the works of Oscar Wilde whom he said he had met in London, adding that he had tried to arbitrate in the growing scandal between Wilde and his lover Alfred Douglas's father.

From multiple accounts one does get the impression of an extreme effeminacy among the boys of that time (counter-balanced by a perhaps smaller group of muscular and tanned lederhosen lads). Years and years later--again drawing from my own year in Berlin--I went home with a boy who seated me in an armchair next to a dimmed lamp. When he sat on the armchair on the other side and leaned towards me the light caught his makeup. In an absolute fit of panic (I was very young) I leaped from the room, jumped down the stairs, and finding the door to the apartment building locked, I shook it like an enraged bull until it broke and I could flee into the street. Needless to say, many of the boys of the 1920s/1930s were not for me, but, of course, there seems to have been many others imminently masculine and virile, for the love of one of whom I spent a year there (11).

Hermann von Teschenberg

Benedict Friedländer

Friedländer (1866 – 1908) had been a member of Hirschfeld's research team but he and like-minded followers formed a dissident group in disgust of Hirschfeld's view that homosexuals were feminine, as well as Ulrichs who made them a weak, effeminate "third sex". For Friedländer's circle, called The Community of the Elite (founded in 1912), homosexuals were not only masculine, but superior in virile qualities to male heterosexuals, a certainty based on historical homosexual heroes from Achilles to Alexander the Great, from Frederick the Great to Jack Nicholson (1) of the Indian Mutiny of 1857, plus an incalculable number of other homosexual warriors (2). Based on Greek man/boy love, the Community worshiped the heroes of Sparta (7), Thebes (8) and Crete, a position that gained popularity among homosexual men who believed themselves to be God's anointed, the chosen few.

Friedländer's views were often esoteric. For example, men of the masses, interested only in material gain and sexual pleasure, turned to women, while men with aesthetic tastes preferred other men. Or this: With the advent of destructive religion priests leagued with women because women were the last refuge of faith in priests, supported by women's belief in superstition and ''mystical terror'', due to a woman's inability to reason. This was supported by Schopenhauer who wrote that one must always guard against women and priests. Because male-male love violated the prerogatives of women and priests, it had to be outlawed. Homosexuals were therefore blamed for earthquakes, pestilence and whatever else could be attributed to homosexual sins against nature (all of which Friedländer brings to us in articles published by *Der Eigene,* some of which can be found in the book by Harry Oosterhuis and Hubert Kennedy *Homosexuality and Male Bonding in Pre-Nazi Germany*, 1991). Friedländer goes on to invoke saints who won the battle over natural drives, ''and in so doing wasted their strength on something insane and useless.'' Success over the mortification of the flesh is the hardest war to win, and the most hollow, a victory for those with the intellect of the rabble, wrote Friedländer. There is little difference between a Christian mortifier and an Indian fakir, and because of Christianity the body was fully covered--even Michelangelo's Sistine Chapel nudes had their genitals painted over (14).

The Community of the Elite folded when Friedländer, struck by a fatal disease, took his own life in Berlin.

Philip Frederick Alexander, Prince of Eulenburg

The life and times of Eulenburg were of extreme importance to the homosexual history of Prussia:

Philip Frederick Alexander, Prince of Eulenburg and Hertefeld, Count of Sandels (1847 – 1921), was born in Prussia to a poor class of nobles. His mother inherited the fortune of an uncle, making the family, overnight, one of the wealthiest in Prussia. Cosima Wagner was a family friend and Eulenburg took part in the cult of Wagner, as did many homosexuals, beginning with King Ludwig II.

He went to a French grammar school in Berlin, French being the language of the German aristocracy. His father obliged him to join the War Academy where he met Count Kuno von Moltke, later exposed for his homosexual engagement with Eulenburg. He studied law at several universities, received a Doctorate of Jurisprudence, *magna cum laude*, from the University of Giessen, and several lovers later he met perhaps the love of his life, the French writer and diplomat Arthur de Gobineau, a racist who convinced Eulenburg that the Prussians/Germans were the Aryan master race, and that he, Gobineau, was a descendant of German Franks. Gobineau later wrote that only Wagner and Eulenburg had been capable of understanding his racist, anti-Semitic views. Somewhere along the way

Eulenburg's love letters to Gobineau were destroyed, as the men of that period did for one another to avoid scandal.

Eulenburg wrote a biographical book about a young man forced into the army by a father incapable of understanding his artistic talents, talents his mother encouraged, becoming ''the ideal figure who filled my whole life with boundless love and fired my inspiration.'' He penned two successful plays and love songs that sold 500,000 copies.

His meeting with Prince Wilhelm of Prussia, during a hunt, changed Eulenburg's life as both fell in love, the prince 12 years younger. Two years later Wilhelm became Emperor Wilhelm II, and Eulenburg remained the most important person in the young Wilhelm's life, although Bismarck, whom Wilhelm had chosen as Chancellor, made sure he became nothing more than the ambassador of the Duchy of Oldenburg. Only to his son did Bismarck reveal that ''His Majesty loved Philip Eulenburg more than any other living being.''

A botched birth left Wilhelm with a withered arm that damaged his self-esteem, and a mother who did not love him sufficiently, perhaps because she felt responsible for his birth defect. The result was a compensating Narcissism in the growing Wilhelm, a Narcissism that Eulenburg's sincere love encouraged. Eulenburg seems to have been incapable of offering anything but sincere love to anyone who came into contact with him, an exception to his times (or any other times).

The plot seriously thickens when the Archduke Rudolf of Austria shot and killed his mistress in what became the Mayerling Incident of 1889, after which he committed suicide. Eulenburg, a rabid enemy of the Catholic church, tried to convince his lover the emperor that this was a scheme by the pope to place Archduke Franz Ferdinand on the throne, after which Austria would unite with France and Russia to destroy Germany, just recently united into one country, as well as German Protestantism. A wait-and-see policy was nonetheless all that could be adopted for the moment by everyone concerned.

Bismarck was eventually dismissed when Eulenburg thought he was planning a *coup d'état* and warned Wilhelm. An old friend of Eulenburg's, Bernard von Bülow, was then named ambassador to Rome, of huge importance because Prussia was now united with Italy under the Triple Alliance (along with Austria), while Eulenburg was named ambassador to Vienna, also of immense importance due to the Double Alliance, Austria and Prussia. (And Eulenburg's old lover Moltke became Wilhelm's aide-de-camp, a position Moltke used to provide Wilhelm with handsome young recruits.) Bülow wrote to Eulenburg, assuring him that in a previous existence they had shared the same body which, when split, gave an effeminate side, Eulenburg, and a masculine entity, Bülow. Eulenburg, Bülow and Wilhelm were all believers in the supernatural. Eulenburg disliked politics because it kept him from fully expressing his artistic talents, and he must have indeed been effeminate in the extreme because the correspondence that circulated between generals and ambassadors referred to him as ''she'', and ''Philine'' instead of Philip. Naturally, thanks to the reciprocal love between Eulenburg and Wilhelm, Eulenburg was now courted by everyone who wanted something, and Bülow, who wanted to be Chancellor, groveled at Eulenburg's feet like no other.

Wilhelm had grown to be a sadist, ordering generals to cross-dress, one made to dance in a pink tutu, another, dressed as a poodle, ordered to bark while he shot off his pistol. Eulenburg called him Darling (*Liebchen*) and rarely Your Majesty. Wilhem surrounded himself with handsome young soldiers and shunned the company of women. As for Eulenburg, he had eight children he adored, although his relations with his wife were described as cold (!). Evidently omnisexual, his preference was nonetheless men and youths.

Eulenburg's troubles began with his younger brother Friedrich, dismissed from the army for homosexuality despite Eulenburg's efforts to have the charges dropped. This was followed, in 1898, by von Moltke's wife filing a complaint against her general husband for having much more sex with Eulenburg than with her. Moltke gave orders to allow his wife to have a divorce that would accord her everything she wished, in exchange for her silence. At the same time a friend wrote Moltke, assuring him of Wilhelm's support, ''The *Liebchen* (Darling Wilhelm) is man enough to stop this nasty gossip against you. He loves you enough in 'your peculiarity' to make sure that not even a shadow of blame will fall upon you.'' The charge of homosexuality nonetheless went through.

In the meantime:

Other events were taking place in China where the Boxer Rebellion broke out in 1900 and the Prussian ambassador von Keteler murdered in public and in cold blood a 14-year-old boy who had nothing to do with the Rebellion. Keteler was himself then killed by Chinese soldiers, which brought on such wrath from Wilhelm that Eulenburg wrote that the emperor had lost his sanity. The anti-Semitic emperor, who hated Orientals and was the first to use the term Yellow Peril, took Keteler's murder as a personal insult. Eulenburg sent a doctor to Wilhelm's side to try to limit the ranting and raving, an appalling scene that became even more appalling when Wilhelm's wife hysterically accused Wilhelm of abandoning both her children and herself for Eulenburg's bed!

Friedrich von Holstein now comes into the picture, a politician partly responsible for getting rid of Bismarck because he wanted Wilhelm to name him Chancellor. As he had great experience, he came to think of himself as indispensible to the kingdom, and when he learned that Wilhelm no longer needed his services, following the advice of Eulenburg who disliked

Holstein, he contacted the journalist Maxmilian Harden to give him information concerning the homosexuality of Eulenburg. Harden published a series of articles about a homosexual clique headed by Eulenburg that had influence over the emperor, and in addition had introduced him to the occult. Harden knew that Eulenburg was having an affair with the First Secretary of the French embassy in Berlin, Gobineau, and was being blackmailed by the French who had forced him to become their spy. The French First Secretary burned his papers, as men all over Europe were now doing who had had intimate contacts with Eulenburg. Harden had worshipped the ultra-virile Bismarck and claimed that men like that were needed to run the country, not soft women or womenish men like Eulenburg. His attacks were so virulent that some historians believe he was putting up a smokescreen to hide his own homosexuality. When Harden stated that Moltke was gay, Moltke sued for libel. It was then that the eminent sexologist Hirschfeld claimed that Moltke was indeed gay, in the hope that this would loosen the laws against homosexuality when one and all saw that even esteemed men like Moltke could be gay, a liberalization that would one day apply to homosexual Hirschfeld himself. When Harden was found innocent, judge Isenbiel ordered a second trial which found him guilty and Harden was obliged to settle the matter out of court.

Von Bülow, who was now Chancellor thanks to having sufficiently kissed Eulenburg's ass, was accused by gay-rights supporter Adolf Brand of being homosexual. Bülow sued Brand, and Eulenburg, accused of being Bülow's lover, testified that homosexuality was a disgusting depravity and should be eradicated without mercy.

From *Der Eigene*, Adolf Brand's publication.

What followed was even more byzantine, if such were possible. Harden paid a Munich journalist to put in print that Eulenburg had solomised two Bavarian fishermen in the 1880s during one of his vacations, and Eulenburg was thusly indicted for perjury because he had claimed under oath in von Bülow's trial that he was not homosexual.

During the trial for perjury it was revealed that Wilhelm II had been with Eulenburg at the time, and that he had been friends of the fishermen. Because emperors rarely frequented such men, it could only be deduced that his interest had been sexual.

The inevitable took place. Eulenburg's *Liebchen* wrote that he wanted nothing to do with homosexuals, and so would never see Eulenburg again, after which Eurenburg became a leper, even to his own family, and it was suggested that be commit suicide to preserve the emperor's honor.

Wilhelm II, whose brain was said to have been as withered as his arm, turned against the only person who truly had loved him, Eulenburg, certainly the only person Wilhelm himself had loved.

Moltke and Eulenburg.

During his trial Eulenburg was confronted by a large number of young working-class men, and when his defense--that it was all a Catholic plot to break up Germany--collapsed, so did Eulenburg, in court. The trial was adjourned because of ill health, and from then on--from 1909 to 1921--he was medically examined twice a year to see if he were fit enough so the trial could go on. In 1921, at age 74, he exited from his (and our) world of hypocrisy.

Sascha Schneider

Rudolf Karl Alexander Schneider (1870 – 1927) was a German painter and sculptor. He lived with his lover, the painter Hellmuth Jahn, but had to flee to Florence when Jahn blackmailed him, threatening to have him arrested under Paragraph 175. He traveled widely with his lover, Robert Speis. For unknown reasons Sascha then financed a voyage for Jahn to Egypt and they met a final time in Florence where Sascha's new lover, Daniel Stepanoff, turned Jahn into the police because he continued to blackmail Sascha. We know that Jahn was in Saxe in 1923, drawing figurines in a porcelain factory. From then on he disappeared from the pages of history. In 1918 Sascha returned to Germany and opened up a bodybuilding gymnasium called the Kraft-Kunst from which he recruited the models for his art (an admittedly genial way of procuring boys, as far as I know unique in the history of artists). He died at age 57 of diabetes.

Sascha Schneider's *Peace on Earth* and unnamed painting.

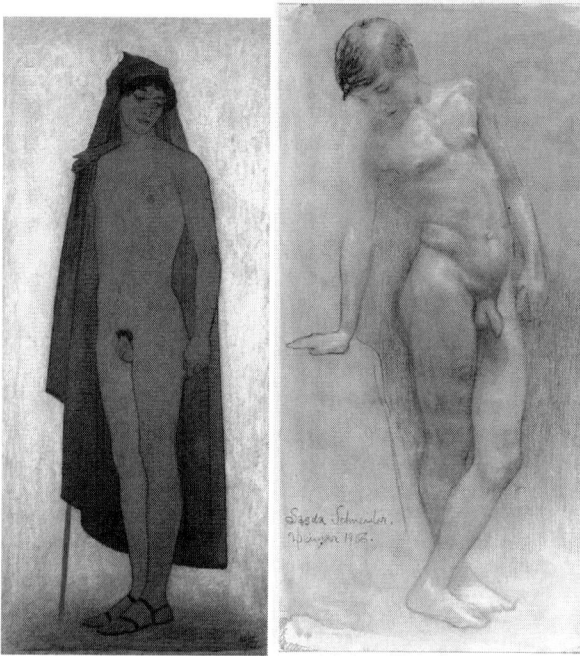

Youth in a Blue Coat and unnamed nude.

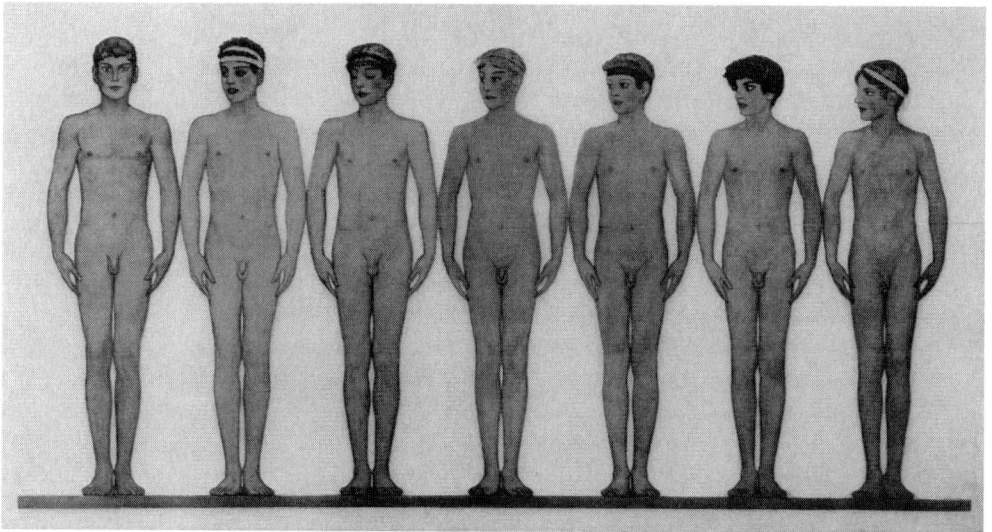

Schneider's *Gymnasium*.

John Henry Mackay

John Henry Mackay (1864 – 1933) was taken to Germany by his well-off mother at the death of his Scottish father when the boy was two. Rebellious and a poor student, his early love affaires were with boys his age,

14 to 17, and although he grew older his preference for adolescent lads did not.

An anarchist, his best-known homosexual work is *The Hustler* (*Der Puppenjung--The Boy-Doll*). His poems were published in *Der Eigene* and he broke with Hirschfeld over Hirschfeld's belief that homosexuals were third-sex-effeminates. Mackay extolled masculinity but unlike many gays he found nothing superior in the love of males to heterosexuals' preferences for girls.

He wrote a series of books called *Nameless Love*, a potpourri of his poems, stories, essays and philosophical beliefs. Judged obscene, his editor--never giving up Mackay's name as the author--was found guilty, but Mackay paid the fines and court costs.

He died in 1933, three months after Hitler's ascension to power, ten days after the Nazi book-burning festival, which saw the destruction of his works (some claim he committed suicide, but this is far from certain).

Max Liebermann

Max Liebermann (1847 – 1935) studied law, philosophy and then art in Paris and the Netherlands. He was a medic in the Franco-Prussian War. His Jewish father had been a banker whose wealth allowed Liebermann to collect French Impressionist art. As well as intellectually supporting Hirschfeld in the abolition of Paragraph 175 he gave solo exhibitions, one at the Prussian Academy in whose ranks he was elected at age 51. Forced out in 1933 by the Nazis, he died in his sleep in 1935. Ordered to a concentration camp in 1943, his bedridden wife committed suicide.

Liebermann's *Im Schwimmbad.*

Glyn Philpot

The British painter Glyn Philpot (1884 – 1937) is of interest to us because he lived in pre-WWII Berlin where he was greatly influenced by the ease of sex with boys, which liberated his painting to the extent that it included male nudes. He joined the Royal Fusiliers where he met Vivian Forbes, described as witty, charming and unstable, the love of Philpot's life despite their union portrayed as tumultuous. Philpot was buried on the 22nd of December 1937 and on the 23rd Forbes took his own life.

Vivian Forbes in Philpot's *Boy with Rabbit* and three other Philpot paintings, the *St. Sebastian* of his lover Heinz Muller.

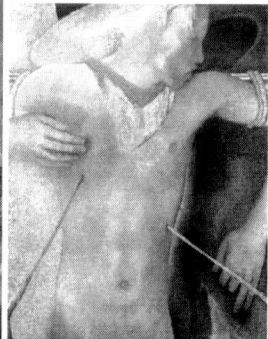

Adolf Brand

Born in Berlin, Adolf Brand (1874 – 1945) founded *Der Eigene, The Special One (*or *The Unique),* the first magazine to celebrate love between men.

Brand, like Friedländer, believed that males were not feminine, nor did they form a third effeminate sex. They were, to the contrary, the peak of masculinity.

Der Eigene boys.

He advocated nudism and outdoor living, love between men and adolescent boys, taking Greece, like Friedländer, as the ultimate aspiration. Both Friedländer and Brand believed that men were bisexual, and both married. Brand served in WWI and wedded a nurse with whom he set up a *ménage-à-trois* with Max Miede who appeared nude in *Der Eigene*.

Max Miede

Der Eigene published--other than nudes--poetry, prose and political manifestos, often in support of Weimar liberality, but always against Paragraph 175. The number of subscribers is unknown, but estimated at 1,500 per issue. There were classified adds, like: student, 22, seeks a real man for friendship ... letter with photograph obligatory, or this: male, 29, seeks an exchange of ideas with a student, *very* pure (my italics), 20 – 25.

In 1933 Brand wrote that the Nazis had a ''hangman's rope in their pockets''. In revenge they raided his home and workshop, destroying everything he had concerning homosexuality, reducing him to extreme poverty. He and his family died in 1945, victims to Allied bombings.

Brand

Accused of being anti-Semitic, in reality he disowned all religions that set up obstacles between men and their rights to love boys. It's true that for him whites were superior and women intellectually inferior, but he was against the exploitation of women and advocated their right to relieve themselves of their burdensome virginity when the occasion presented itself. The focal point of his life was best summed up in his own words: ''The right of self-determination over body and soul is the most important basis of all freedom.''

Brand grew to hate Hirschfeld, and not only because Hirschfeld thought homosexuals were third-sex effeminates, but especially because Hirschfeld failed to help him in Brand's time of need. The story is convoluted. The reader remembers that Hirschfeld intervened in the trial of Eulenburg by claiming that General Moltke was homosexual, something Hirschfeld could recognize thanks to his long and thorough research into homosexuality (said he). Hirschfeld wanted Moltke to be labeled gay so that homosexuality would be recognized as something shared by even the most virile of men, and should therefore be accepted by all, the end product of which would be the abrogation of Paragraph 175.

When Brand saw all the publicity Hirschfeld received, and the boon that it was to Hirschfeld's Institute, bringing in money and new members, he decided to do the same thing by accusing Wilhelm II's Chancellor Bernard von Bülow of being homosexual, which was true, but known to only a few. Von Bülow sued him for libel and Hirschfeld was called to testify against von Bülow. But this time Hirschfeld's reception of ''homosexual-revealing waves'' didn't work (although Hirschfeld knew von Bülow was as homosexual as Hirschfeld was himself). Perhaps Hirschfeld refused because he was tired of making highly placed enemies, or perhaps he was tired of ruining peoples' lives by outing them. The end result was that Brand was found guilty of libel and sent to prison for 18 months.

Brand did not only defend Greek love, he wished to bring Ancient Greece to Berlin in its entirety. He founded an organization called, modestly, the Community of the Special, that had regular meetings dubbed symposiums after Brand's conception of what went on in the Athenian agora. The Community was prone to nature hikes in the nude, and was built on the principle of love between a man and the boy the man would better through education, and this until the boy was old enough to marry, after which the boy, now a man, would find a boy he could, in turn, love and educate--Greece at its most classic.

Brand was the antitheses of Hirschfeld whose teas and nocturnal sorties were love fests. He was highly strung, touchy, and could be violent, as when he attacked an official with a whip. His run-ins with the police were never-ending, and *Der Eigene* was often confiscated for the naked boys it presented and its erotic literary content. So he came up with the idea of having the Community of the Special changed into a *private* organization whose members subscribed to his publications, making them untouchable by the authorities.

His boys eventually married, as he did himself, which in no way stopped him from having multiple lovers, a perfect life only an allied bomb could put an end to. If Brand's life were really so wonderful cannot be known, in the same way that Thomas Mann's personal life (briefly described elsewhere in this book) was, on the exterior, one of wealth (gorgeous homes and chauffeured cars) and respect (a Nobel Prize and a chair at Princeton University) but included too a loveless marriage to a rich woman when Mann was himself poor, incestuous longing for his son Klaus and his daughter Elizabeth, suicides galore, along with his retched abandonment of his boys Michael and Golo.

Brand started the *Extrapost*, full of personal ads for which he had to pay fines for ''soliciting'', followed by *Friendship and Freedom* and *Eros*, a successful magazine that brought in personal ads from countries as far ranged as America, Sweden and Russia. Memberhip in his Community of the Special increased to an estimated 1,500, with the side benefit of a much younger new boyfriend, Max Miede, as reported.

Brand favored loving, sexually satisfying relationships as opposed to the animal couplings of the Tiergarten. Self-pleasuring was discouraged, as were *female* prostitutes, carriers of disease, and premarital heterosexual intercourse. Boys were free to do whatever they wanted, as long as the eroticism was among themselves. As with the Ancient Greeks, there could be no harm attached to the finality of love between males, built on exercise, education and reciprocal ejaculation.

Some of Röhm's fascists worked with Brand against the Jew Hirschfeld, supplying *Der Eigene* with articles and cartoons ridiculing Hirschfeld, calling him an aunt, the German *tante* (fairy) being a highly derogative word for the effeminate (passive) element of a homosexual couple. One of Röhm's boys, Karl-Günther Heimsoth, worked closely with Brand. During the Night of the Long Knives Röhm, his lover Karl-Günther Heimsoth and an estimated 85 others were murdered.

Karl-Günther Heimsoth (1899 – 1934) served in the Prussian army and on the Western Front until 1918. He became a medical doctor in 1924 and penned a dissertation *Heterophile and Homophile*. He wrote that a masculine man could want another masculine man, his emphasis on *masculine*, separating him from Hirschfeld and his dainty third-sex cross-dressers. He wrote articles in Brand's *Der Eigene* stressing what was heroic and virile in homoerotic friendships, and asked former soldiers and leaders of youth movements to send him examples of their own experiences in homoerotic love.

Heimsoth's relationship with Röhm started out through letters he sent to Röhm who was in prison because of his participation in the Munich Beer Hall Putsch. When Röhm was freed they attended meetings together, the center point being the abrogation of Paragraph 175. He was active in the Nazi Party but then joined the communist Party for whom he spied, one reason he was one of the first to die during the Night of the Long Knives, but also because, thanks to Röhm, he knew where the Nazi leaders' skeletons were buried.

Brand also published magazines of nude youths: *Journal for Nudism* (*Blätter fur Nachtkultur*) and *Race and Beauty* (*Rasse und Schönheit*). He wanted to found a series of open-air nudist sports camps, but in the end lacked the funds (certainly because investors feared being outed).

Another publication, the first homosexual magazine openly sold at newsstands, was *Die Freundschaft* (1919 – 1933), edited by Georg Plock. It covered the history of homosexuality in articles, as well as reasons for the repeal of Paragraph 175. It favored spiritualism, reincarnation and karma, had personal advertisements, photographs and art. It was at first published weekly, then monthly, and finally semi-annually. It was considered expensive at 50 pfennig, the cost of a soldier or sailor.

Brand published pictures by Wilhelm von Gloeden:

Sicilian boys by Wilhelm von Gloeden.

Wilhelm von Gloeden had gone to the island of Sicily for his health. His guide was a 16-year-old donkey driver with whom he spent a night in such ecstasy, he wrote, that he bought a villa and hired local 13- and 14-year-olds to staff it. The boys' parents competed in having their lads work for him as he paid well, he took scrupulous care of their health and needs, he turned over the royalties from the photos he took of them, and he provided dowries so that his favorites could marry. His character was such that everyone sought him out. His orgies became famous and visitors to them were said to have been in the hundreds (presumably not all at the same time). Frederick von Krupp was one, who later tried to recreate Taormina on Capri. When his homosexuality came to light, he is supposed to have put a bullet in his head, although his death was masked as a heart attack. Gloeden was noted as the first man to use filters and body make-up, said to have been composed of milk, glycerin, olive oil and perfume. He left his negatives to his lover, Il Moro, whom he had ''known'' at age 13. He at times worked with his cousin, Guglielmo Plüschow, an avid boy-lover said to have been less talented and more stilted in his posing of the lads. Some people at Taormina, today, claim that the origin of their wealth is a heritage from the sums given to their grandsons.

Il Moro and Gloeden.

Der Eigene

Many articles sent to *Der Eigene* were not erotically motivated. One man, for example, questioned the utility of Paragraph 175, two parts of which made crimes of having consensual sex with underage boys, as well as the rape of boys. But the laws were in existence already concerning girls (Paragraphs 176, 177 and 182) and all that was needed, according to the writer of the article, was to change ''girls'' to ''persons''. The writer went on to state that laws had four main goals: 1) Atonement; but what atonement was necessary when the act of love took place between two consenting adults? 2) Determent; but no law would ever put a halt to acts of love [which even burning at the stake didn't deter from the Middle Ages to the Enlightenment]. 3) Reformation; but reforming homosexuals was impossible because such was their unalterable nature. And 4) rendering the criminal harmless; but the act of love between men was already harmless, so how could one make something harmless still more harmless? On the other hand, the writer concludes, Paragraph 175 opened the way to blackmailers, in effect inventing a whole new breed of criminals who used male prostitutes to entrap and bleed dry homosexuals, not to mention the resultant suicides.

Another article in *Der Eigene*, brought to us by Oosterhuis and Kennedy, signed by Heinrich Pudor, concerns the Greek ideal of the human body, one that had the body itself as the seat of life and not just the brain, a body exposed to all and not just the face as is the case today where clothing covers most of the body surface, a Greek body that one could look on without prudery because it had always been unveiled, a body enjoyed as often outdoors as in, in forests and along streams. In Greece there was no nudity in art because men were always nude, no unhealthy desire to spy on one taking off his shirt or perhaps lowering his trousers, because in Greece one was as often naked as dressed. And when we do paint or sculpt nudes, Pudor goes on to say, they are not the healthy boys of the gymnasiums but hustlers bought on the street.

Christianity turned the beautiful work of God ''into a Hell and a cesspool of sin, the body one hides in clothes or under blankets, even when married.'' Pudor concludes by saying that even the nudes of Titian and Rembrandt are flesh and no spirit, no intellect, nothing of a charming nature, ''not human in the Greek sense'' (although he does make an exception for Dürer, as well as Michelangelo who saw ''man the human, down to the bones and into the life cells and sex cells'').

Oosterhuis and Kennedy brought us an article found in *Der Eigene* that concerns the destiny of boys between the ages of 15 and 30, 15 being the time he awakens sexually and 30 the age at which he marries. During the 15 year hiatus the lad has three sexual outlets: 1) He can go with a prostitute and become victim to gonorrhea and/or syphilis, he can 2) seduce a respectable girl, the end result being his paying for child support throughout the rest of his life when the inevitable happens; he also ruins the girl's reputation and, abandoned, sends her into the arms of pimps. 3) He can masturbate, a practice known to all boys but inherently unsatisfactory and unhealthy if practiced in the extreme. The natural solution to the boy/man's problem came about 2,000 years before, when a boy was taken under the protective shield of an older man, educated and given natural, loving sexual relief. The Greek boy would then marry and take a boy of his own, while his wife prepared the male couple's meals and bore their children (Heracles presented his boy Iolaus, then age sixteen, to his wife, age thirty, with whom he had a child). This was the Greek solution, continues the writer, thanks to which we know the Greeks were far in advance of us. The article ends by stating that the road to the Greek way can only be cleared through the abrogation of Paragraph 175.

In an article by Adolf Brand himself he claims that love must be a private affair just as religion is, and that laws against it are shameless crimes against personal freedom, and that nothing is worse than punishment for "the joys of friendship and friend-love", state Oosterhuis and Kennedy in their translation of the *Der Eigene* text. Brand goes on to defend the innocent girl, arguing that boys should leave them alone because by bedding them the boy destroys their reputations while obliging them to bare illegitimate children the state must pay to educate, clothe and feed. Brand assures us that these heinous acts are taking place in the thousands per day, disgusting immorality that could be immediately alleviated if boys--in my personal interpretation of what he wrote--were allowed to spill their seed on male abdomens or in male orifices. "Nature has allowed some of us to know the joy of male hearts and spirit, the admiration of male strength and beauty, the respect for male freedom and greatness, the deeply sensual and strongly spiritual love for one's own sex. Without that feeling of desire and without its constant satisfaction, which is willed by nature, all civilization and all progress on earth would simply be impossible." Love between males, continues Brand, also frees boys from searching out sexual satisfaction with girls until the boys are intellectually and economically ready to raise a family, thusly freeing the girl from disgrace and disgraceful abortions. The lad is also spared from visiting prostitutes and the accompanying diseases. "Love of a friend allows one to grow beyond one's self with his heart and soul, to bring into the world deeds of noble-mindedness and self-sacrifice, bestowing honor and glory on the love and passion inherent with the same sex. It is the wish to live with and for the other, to think about him and to work for him; to educate him, to promote him, to raise him up; to shape existence into something bearable; to take delight with him in this beautiful world."

Brand maintained "that all great men throughout history have devoted themselves to friend-love," namely Alexander the Great, Caesar, Frederick the Great, Socrates, Nietzsche, Plato, Virgil, Goethe, Schiller, Michelangelo," and others. Friend-love has founded schools and gymnasiums, temples and churches, monasteries and knightly orders, "all carried out by chosen beautiful boys. Every young man contested with his peers to show himself ever more love worthy and desirable, so as to be loved by the hero of his soul and conquer his lasting friendship."

Brand accepts as normal that in the end a boy must marry, that he expresses in this way, again brought to us by Kennedy and Oosterhuis: "Sexual satisfaction of young lads and men among themselves is no sin, but rather a clever outlet of nature in time of puberty, which is a transition to *genuine* sexual intercourse (my italics). Every German friend should choose for himself a friend of whom he can openly boast in the circle of his comrades and to whom he swears loyalty, until the time when he marries or when death separates the two. It is the only salvation from the frightfully lewd and dissolute life of the post-war period" (post-WWI).

An article in *Der Eigene* stated that the foundations of Christianity resembled those of early Rome where the Romans ''built temple after temple, cheered on by the masses who had no inkling of the destructive powers of Christianity on the horizon.'' Now it is Christianity that is shaken by the Enlightenment and would soon have a final showdown with rising science. ''Everything is in ferment, from the slight doubts of the schoolboy who is told the world was created in seven days,'' to Nietzsche who declared that as a child he had not been childish enough to succumb to silly religions.

The writer goes on to express the need for two things before Germans can go on the offensive against religious intolerance. The first is that homosexuals have to clean up their show. ''Anyone can go to Friedrichstrasse and pick up a boy. Nothing easier. But in that case homosexuality lowers itself to the gutter where one finds female whores, which is a stain that must be removed. The second thing that must be done is the repeal of Paragraph 175 so that the fight can take place on a level field. The end result will be ''our civilization will become higher and more splendid. The summery culture of ancient Hellas will renew itself. We will attain the goal of being publicly allowed to court and return love and friendship.'' When this takes place fathers will no longer warn their sons against relations with men, but will encourage the relations because the youths will be educated and improved by the men. Boys will no longer be afraid of the bisexualism within them but ''allow the fulfillment of their inner homosexual drive'', and our athletic fields will play a role as in the palaestra and gymnasiums of Athens. And sexual intercourse will replace solitary masturbation, the real enemy of virtue and health. And because boys will give their love freely, male prostitution will vanish. Finally, as men will cease to consider women as only sexual objects, women will gain a nobler and happier level.

Paragraph 175 of the Penal Code

Germany was unified in 1871, as related earlier, and that same year Paragraph 175 was enacted, making homosexual acts between men illegal. It was repealed in 1994 only, years after the fall of Nazi Germany. Between 1871 and 1994 an estimated 140,000 men were convicted for lewd acts. The paragraph was reinforced by the Nazis in 1935 to include masturbating side by side, and between 5,000 to 15,000 homosexuals were sent to concentration camps, few of whom left alive. Between 1945 and 1969 the age of consent for homosexual acts was set at 21, lowered to 18 in 1973 and 14 in 1994, along with the repeal of Paragraph 175. *East* Berlin had been far more lenient as of 1968.

Friedrich Radszuweit

Friedrich Radszuweit (1876 – 1932) was a Berlin homosexual activist who published mildly erotic magazines and books he himself wrote. He too sought to overturn Paragraph 175. Radszuweit published *Die Freundschaft* from 1919 until the reign of the Nazis in 1933. It was by far the most successful publication, selling an estimated 15,000 copies at each printing, making Radszuweit rich, especially when this income was supplemented by ads from not only bars, cafés and clubs, but also from men's clothing shops, barbers and doctors whose discretion homosexuals relied on for anal disorders as well as, Beachy says, ''throat rashes''. Radszuweit founded the Theater of Eros, known for the homosexual content of its plays and deep kissing between male actors on stage. Like Adolf Brand, Radszuweit's brand of homosexuality included virile males only, with no place whatsoever for Hirschfeld's cross-dressing effeminates. Radszuweit differed sharply from Brand in his belief that males were entirely attracted to and satisfied by other males, which excluded bisexuality, and that boys were to be protected, which was not the case under Brand where boys were meant to be dominated and educated by mature, responsible men. Radszuweit did believe in Brand's assertion that only between males could one find the highest degree of moral strength, spiritual calm and sexual release.

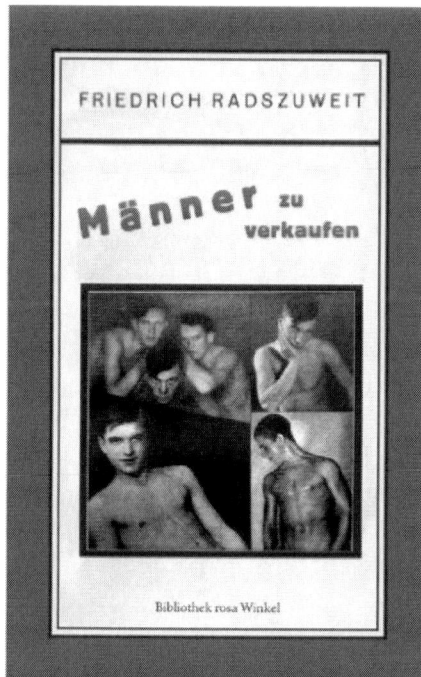

FRIEDRICH RADSZUWEIT

Männer zu verkaufen

Bibliothek rosa Winkel

His magazine *Männer*.

His lover was Martin Butzko, an active member of the Hitler Youth whom he adopted as his son. Martin-Butzko Radszuweit took over the publishing company when his "father" died in 1932, but the establishment was raided and destroyed by the Nazis in 1933. Hirschfeld's Institute and estate were destroyed at the same time and Hirschfeld himself died in France in 1935 at the age of 67, his faithful lover Giese presumably at his side.

Henry Gerber

Henry Gerber (1892 – 1972) was born in Bavaria and emigrated to America at age 21. When war broke out with Germany he was given the choice of being interned or of joining the American Army. He chose the Army and was sent to Coblenz for three years as a printer and proofreader. It was there he learned about Hirschfeld and became his acolyte, adopting, alas, Hirschfeld's idea that homosexuals were just naturally effeminate. Back in the States he worked at the post office in Chicago. He founded the first homosexual organization in America, the Society of Human Rights, the goal of which was: "to promote and protect the interests of people who by reasons of mental and physical abnormalities are abused and hindered in the legal pursuit of happiness which is guaranteed them by the Declaration of Independence." As homosexuals were the "mental and physical abnormalities" he defended, we can be grateful for the fact that the Society had an early death, in a way that was almost hilarious: He decided to limit the Society to exclusively homosexuals (we don't know why), apparently unaware that his vice-president had two children. The vice-president's wife called the police who put Gerber on trial *three times* for being a degenerate.

The charges were eventually dismissed but Gerber lost his life savings in lawyers' fees and the bribes it was necessary to pay out at the time (it being, after all, Chicago). He was fired from the post office for "conduct unbecoming...."

He met up with an old army pal who suggested he reenlist, which he did, preparing magazines and recruiting publications for the Army Recruiting Bureau. He retired in 1945 and for the next thirty years was an active part of the N.Y. gay scene, also corresponding with groups around the country and in Germany. He entered the Soldiers' and Airmens' Home in Washington D.C. where he died at age 80 in 1972.

Although not a single rich Chicago homosexual offered Gerber a penny for his defense during his trial, they've made up for it since then. The Henry Gerber House where he had started the Society of Human Rights became an official Chicago Landmark in 2001 and then a National Historic Landmark just last year, in 2015. Gerber was enrolled in the Chicago Gay and Lesbian Hall of Fame. Too bad that Gerber passed away far too soon to reap the rewards for his courage.

Thomas Mann

Thomas Mann's early years were exclusively homosexual, his first love and lover the schoolboy Armin Martins he immortalized in his book *Tonio Kröger*:

Thomas Mann and his first love Armin Martens,
hero of Mann's book *Tonio Kröger*.

A second unnamed boyhood love is thought to have been the inspiration behind the hero of his *Magic Mountain*, Hans Castorp.

The love of his life was perhaps Paul Ehrenberg, a violinist and impressionist painter:

Paul Ehrenberg--with my apologies for the terrible image. Of his four years of love with Paul he wrote, "I have lived and loved. I knew happiness, held in my arms he I longed for." To my mind the very aim of life. The *only* aim of life.

At age 53 he fell in love with Klaus Heuser, 17:

Klaus Heuser

And at age 75 he loved a young Zurich waiter, Franz Westermeier (no photo available), around whom he wrote *The Confessions of Felix Krull*. When tracked down in N.Y. Westermeier said that he and Mann had spent their time together in polite conversation, which led some of Mann's biographers to state that Mann had been unable to "conclude" all his life, which is ridiculous. He perhaps couldn't go farther due to his age, but it's possible too he didn't want to subject Westermeier to his withered body. Three volumes of Mann's dairies have come out, followed by three major biographies, revealing little of a sexual nature, leaving some biographers to wonder if he perhaps died a virgin to homosexuality. That he was heterosexual, producing six children during fifty years of marriage, had one writer remark, amusingly, that "he had gone beyond the call of duty." Mann died at age 80.

Death in Venice, like his other books, reflected true-life experiences, this one taking place at the Grand Hôtel des Bains on the Lido of Venice in the summer of 1911. After *Death in Venice* came out the boy-hero of the book recognized himself and went wild, shouting out to one and all, That's me! That's me! Władysław Moes' story is of incidental interest. Born in 1900 (he died at age 88), he was at the Grand Hôtel des Bains in 1911 during a visit by Mann, who published his book in 1922. Władysław Moes was born into a Polish family of extremely rich industrialists. He lost everything with the Communist takeover and earned his living as a translator. In an interview to the Polish translator of Mann's works he said, "Even in Venice they called me Adzio, and in the story I'm Tadzio, which is how the Master understood it."

There are numerous theories as to why Thomas married, his many biographers suggest that his wife's family was rich and as a young writer he was poor, or that he wanted to punish himself for his homosexuality, or that he capitulated to convention, sacrificing his true nature in order to protect his public image.

Thomas Mann taught at Princeton before moving to California, and spent the last three years of his life in Switzerland.

Klaus Mann (1906 – 1949)

Perhaps only the Borgias come close to the Manns in accusations of incest, Pope Alexander VI being both the father and lover of his son Cesare and the father and lover to his daughter Lucrezia. Cesare was the lover of his sister Lucrezia, and one novel has Alexander encouraging his son to enter Lucrezia more tenderly because she complains that Cesare is being too rough (12).

Klaus Mann's father Thomas--the 1919 Noble Prize winner for literature--was himself homosexual. He gave birth to three homosexual children, a daughter Erika, and his two sons Klaus and Golo were homosexually involved: "I heard a noise from the boys' room and surprised Issi,"--Thomas Mann's nickname for his son Klaus--"completely naked, in front of Golo's bed doing silly things. Strong impression of his startling and already almost virile body, what a shock!" wrote Thomas, which was part of his book *Joseph and His Brothers*, followed by his book *Disorder and Early Sorrow* about his own incest with his daughter Elizabeth. Thomas may well have had incestuous relations with Klaus: "Eissi terribly handsome in his swimsuit"--the boy being 14--"deeply struck by his radiant adolescent body", "Read a story to Eissi yesterday ... while lavishing caresses on him which pleased him, I believe", and "I find it quite natural to fall in love with my own son." Mann goes on about his wife's incest with her brother in *Blood of the Walsungs* and Klaus wrote about his own incest with his sister Erika in *The Siblings* (incest with his brother Golo was probably considered too normal to be commented on in a book).

Klaus Mann

In 1919, just after the war, the Manns were so poor that a remaining fig was deeply desired by Mann's six children. He gave it to Erika, telling the children that it was time they learned that life was unjust (which Mann himself found out when he was forced to flee Germany, his summer house on the Baltic stolen by Göring).

Wealthy later on, the Manns were chauffeured to the theater, and the enormous prestige of the prizes Thomas won perhaps played its part in his belief that he and his family were well above conventional bourgeois morality. Thomas did not hide his dislike for his two sons Golo and Michael, Michael who committed suicide. Klaus became a US citizen in 1945 and died in Cannes of a sleeping-pill overdose in 1949, followed by Michael's suicide in 1977 in California, Michael a renowned violinist and professor of literature.

Perhaps Thomas Mann himself didn't know why he neglected both Golo and Michael, why he would beat them both and, in the end, turn against Klaus too, hitting him with his cane as did Frederick the Great's father. The irony is that the man who loved boys ended up respecting only his two daughters, Erika and Elizabeth. (In 1926 Klaus married Pamela Wedeking, Erika's lover, and Erika married Gustaf Gründgens, a homosexual actor; they all eventually divorced.)

Happily Erika, who favored girls, and Klaus, who slept with boys, formed an indestructible love from their very childhood, sharing even a bedroom.

Klaus and Erika

Golo Mann

The name Golo came from the young boy's own pronunciation of his name, Angelus Gottfried Thomas Mann (1909 – 1994). A historian and writer, adept in Latin, he was a citizen of the world, holding nationalities in Germany, Czechoslovakia, America and Switzerland. He studied law in Munich and graduated in philosophy at the University of Heidelberg. After his parents left Germany in 1933 he saw to it that three of his remaining brothers and sisters got out safely and then smuggled what was left of the family fortune to Switzerland. He taught German in the prestigious French Ecole Normale Supérieure and then joined his father in Switzerland where he helped edit his diaries. Relations between father and son improved but Golo nonetheless wrote: ''It was inevitable that I wished his death, but I was completely broken hearted when it came to pass.''

He joined the Czech army in France in 1940 to fight against the Germans. Taken captive, he later escaped, crossed the Alps and made it to Lisbon where he took a boat to N.Y. city. Along with his brother Klaus he joined the US Army in 1943 as a translator. In 1947 he became a professor of history at the Clarement Men's College that he called ''the happiest nine years of my life'' even if he found the students ''painfully stupid''. He published a best seller, *German History of the 19th and 20th Century* and went on to teach at different universities--Münster, Stuttgart and others, and received an honorary degree from the University of Bath. He was even a ghost writer for Willy Brandt.

He adopted his lover who became Hans Beck-Mann in 1955, but who died in 1986, followed by Golo himself in 1994. About his homosexuality he said, ''I did not fall in love often. I often kept it to myself. It was forbidden, even in America, and one had to be a little careful.'' Despite today's liberality in the United States (2016), one still has to be a little careful.

The Wandervogel Movement

The Wandervogel movement (1896 – 1933), a name most likely taken from Walt Whitman's ''Birds of Passage'', sprang up in Berlin when high school students turned their walks through the forests into an antibourgeois back-to-nature group based on hiking, swimming, camping, singing and story telling, most often in tents or barns, in the nude. The conversations around campfires were on how to make Germany and Europe a better place. It was homoerotic, but only in the sense that male-male love was a simple, natural aspect of manhood. It gave meaning to a German boy's life, in which friendship and camaraderie became a cult. Around the year 1900 it had 26,000 members.

''A one-sided cultivation of the body is as wrong as the exclusive education of the intellect. One creates healthy, robust blockheads; the other flabby, bent scholars. The Golden Mean is a sound mind in a sound body.'' Wandervogel philosophy.

In 1931 Hans Blüher organized a subdivision of the Wandervogel, one for men only, based on male bonding. His movement was publicized by Adolf Brand's *Der Eigene.* Blüher based his ideas on male cohesion as shown through the Spartans (7) and the Sacred Band of Thebes (8), Hadrian and Antinous (6) and, of course, Wagner and his *Persifal.*

Homosexuality was a natural phenomenon in sexuality, as were other forms, so that exclusively homosexual attachments were in no way obligatory in Blüher's Wandervogel. But as the journalist Ludwig Lewisohn wrote in 1933, the Wandervogel was ''the youth movement from which thousands of stormtroopers came, its ideology drenched through with homoerotic feeling *and practice''*, my italics. The Wandervogel and all other youth movements were incorporated into the Hitler Youth in 1933.

''No young man should marry before he has seen his beloved in the nude, just as he sees his comrades in the nude. Nudism elevates the pleasure of every individual and the joy of our whole people in bodily strength and beauty.'' Adolf Brand.

The Wondervogel movement was influenced by Richard Ungewitters' books, all on nudism (naturalism today) which recommended going nude as a way of keeping healthy (clothes being the breeders of tuberculosis, maintained Ungewitters), especially as nudists were advised to do a lot of healthy hiking. Women could visually see the attributes of virile males, meaning a strengthening of the race because weaklings would not be chosen in reproduction. He wrote that exercising three times a day should be made obligatory. Ungewitters was anti-Semitic, perhaps in part due to the absence of Jewish boys' foreskins. Since ancient times it was considered obscene to expose the penis glans, so in Greece a precaution was to tie up the end of the foreskin with a string that was attacked to the base of the penis at the bush (11). Circumcised Jews were not allowed to participate in Greek games because of the exposed glans. To overcome the ban the Jews attached weights to what remained of their foreskins, producing a new foreskin over time. Some resorted to surgery, but many died from the resulting infections.

Hans Blüher

Hans Blüher (1888 – 1955) started out in the Wandervogel at age 14 but received a dressing-down for homosexual activity. He met Wilhelm Jansen, a member of Hirschfeld's committee and he and Friedländer encouraged Blüher's homosexuality--Blüher then 18--which was easy as Blüher had been making love with boys since puberty. He married, a passionless love known to boys on both sides of the Channel, the British too succumbing to bourgeois normality and societal demands. He adopted Freud's theory that we are all born innately bisexual, which comforted Blüher in his love of boys and later marriage. Blüher admitted one exception to bisexuality, that of ''super-virile homosexuals'' who have physical contacts with men only. For Blüher physical contacts between men were both positive and good. Blüher believed that friendship and erotic love were the norm between men, while Hirschfeld thought that heterosexuals could love men as friends only.

Blüher rightly claimed that before Christianity muddied the waters, love between men was a simple aspect of manhood, not a special condition of man.

Arno Breker

Arno Breker (1900 – 1991) was a German sculptor whose prizes, awarded by the Prussian Ministry of Culture, allowed him to live in Paris and Rome.

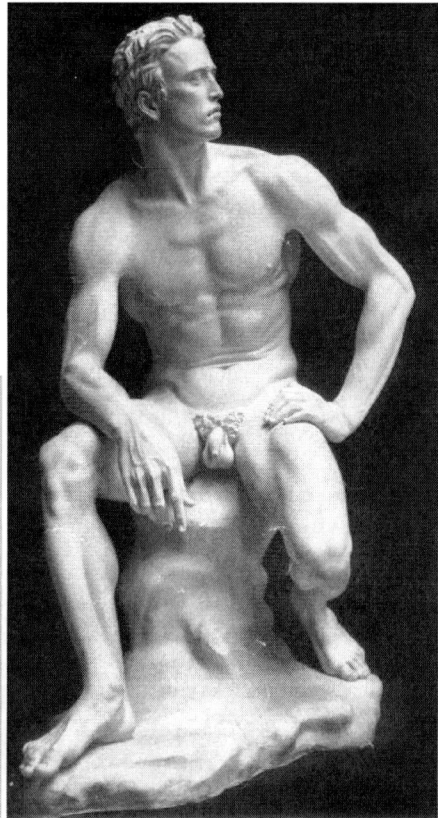

Breker and his *Alexander the Great* and *Seated Man.*

Called ''Germany's Michelangelo'' by the sculptor and painter Aristide Maillol, he was friends with Picasso, Jean Renoir, Albert Speer and Hitler, all of whom appreciated his muscular and flawlessly handsome

Aryan sculptures. Although his escaped allied bombing, the occupational forces nonetheless destroyed nearly all of his oeuvre.

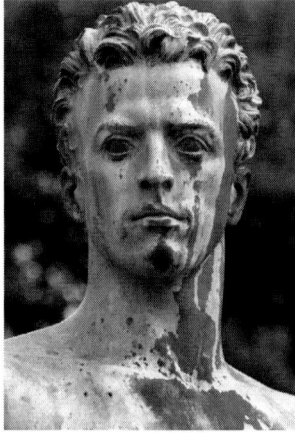

Young Man.

When offered work by Stalin, Breker declined with ''One dictator was enough!'' Rehabilitated, the Arno Breker Museum was inaugurated in 1985.

PART VIII

PRUSSIAN INSPIRATION

HERMAN MELVILLE – *THE PRUSSIAN OFFICER*

1819 - 1891

Herman Melville's story *The Prussian Officer* recounts the life and death of a Prussian officer whose repressed love for his orderly pushes him to be more and more sadistic with the boy, humiliating him in words and attitude, until becoming maddened to the point of throwing a belt at him, bloodying the boy's mouth, and then kicking him, until: ''The spur of the officer caught in a tree-root, he went down backwards with a crash, the middle of his back thudding sickeningly against a sharp-edged tree-base, the pot flying away. And in a second the orderly, with serious, earnest young face, and under-lip between his teeth, had got his knee in the officer's chest and was pressing the chin backward over the farther edge of the tree-stump, pressing, with all his heart behind in a passion of relief, the tension of his wrists exquisite with relief. And with the base of his palms he shoved at the chin, with all his might. And it was pleasant, too, to have that chin, that hard jaw already slightly rough with beard, in his hands. He did not relax one hair's breadth, but, all the force of all his blood exulting in his thrust, he shoved back the head of the other man, till there was a little cluck and a crunching sensation. Then he felt as if his head went to vapour. Heavy convulsions shook the body of the officer, frightening and horrifying the young soldier. Yet it pleased him, too, to repress them. It pleased him to keep his hands pressing back the chin, to feel the chest of the other man yield in expiration to the weight of his strong, young knees, to feel the hard twitchings of the prostrate body jerking his own whole frame, which was pressed down on it.

"But it went still. He could look into the nostrils of the other man, the eyes he could scarcely see. How curiously the mouth was pushed out, exaggerating the full lips, and the moustache bristling up from them. Then, with a start, he noticed the nostrils gradually filled with blood. The red brimmed, hesitated, ran over, and went in a thin trickle down the face to the eyes."

Melville

Various excerpts reveal the homoerotic nature of the story: "He was a Prussian aristocrat, haughty and overbearing. Having made too many gambling debts when he was young ... no woman had ever moved him. His orderly, having to rub him down, admired the amazing riding-muscles of his loins ... a handsome figure in pale blue uniform with facings of scarlet.... To his orderly he was at first cold and just and indifferent. Then the change gradually came. The orderly was a youth of about twenty-two, well built ... swarthy, with a soft, black, young moustache. There was something altogether warm and young about him.... And yet as the young soldier moved unthinking about the apartment, the elder watched him, and would notice the movement of his strong young shoulders under the blue cloth, the bend of his neck. And it irritated him. To see the soldier's young, brown, shapely peasant's hand grasp the loaf or the wine-bottle ... it was rather the blind, instinctive sureness of movement of an unhampered young animal that irritated the officer to such a degree.... He hated those fine, black brows, dark eyes, he was infuriated by the free movement of the handsome limbs, which no military discipline could make stiff. And he became harsh and cruelly bullying, using contempt and satire. The young soldier only grew more mute and expressionless.... Once he flung a heavy military glove into the young soldier's face. Then he had the satisfaction of seeing the black eyes flare up into his own, like a blaze when straw is thrown on a fire. And he had laughed with a little tremor and a sneer.... The officer tried hard not to admit the passion that had got hold of him.... At last he slung the end of a belt in his servant's face. When he saw the youth start back, the pain-tears in his eyes and the blood on his mouth, he had felt at once a thrill of deep pleasure and of shame.... He watched the strong, easy young figure, the fine eyebrows, the thick black hair. In a week's time the youth had got back his old well-being. The hands of the officer twitched and seemed to be full of mad flame.''

Melville's father, of French origin, provided the boy with an excellent schooling and digs with servants until his death from pneumonia when the boy was 13, obliging him to enter his uncle's bank at age 14. Thanks to inheritances he was able to continue his schooling later on, and throughout his entire adolescence he was an avid reader, books which apparently inspired his later writing, as he took notes of his favorite passages and descriptions. He prized public speaking and debates, and two early works of his, on politics, made it into the papers, at age 19. Inspired by the book *Two Years Before the Mast* he signed on as a ''green hand'' on the whaler *Acushnet* for 1/175th of the profits, remuneration then in practice, used even on pirate ships. He deserted in the Marquises Islands and spent time island hopping until enlisting on the *USS United States*, his experiences written up in his books *Typee, Omoo* and *White-Jacket.*

Because his books didn't sell well, and some critics wrote humiliating reviews, he was obliged to work as a customs inspector for the city of N.Y. He had confided to his intimate friend Hawthorne that he contemplated suicide, a choice his son Malcolm took at age 18, at the end of a shotgun. His second son Stanwix died at age 36 of illness. Melville himself died at age 72 in 1891. Around 1930 there began a Melville revival, the epicenter of which was Yale University.

ARTISTS OF UNKNOWN SEXUALITY

Joseph Thorak (1889 – 1952) was a Bavarian sculptor of the grandiose. His *Comradeship* adorned the German pavilion at the Paris World's Fair in 1889, and other statues, up to 65' (20 meters) high were present at the Berlin Olympics of 1936. Albert Speer who called Thorak ''my sculptor''.

Georg Kolbe (1877 – 1947) sculpted for the Nazis who prized his nudes but supposedly refused to sculpt a head of Hitler. He did sculpt Franco and was hailed by Goebbels.

Richard Scheibe (1879 – 1964) is responsible for the national emblem known as the *Hoheitszeichen* as well as the sculpture on the cover of this book. Nearly nothing is known about his life.

Albert Janesch painted his *Water Sports* for the 1936 Berlin Olympics. His paintings were privately collected by Hitler.

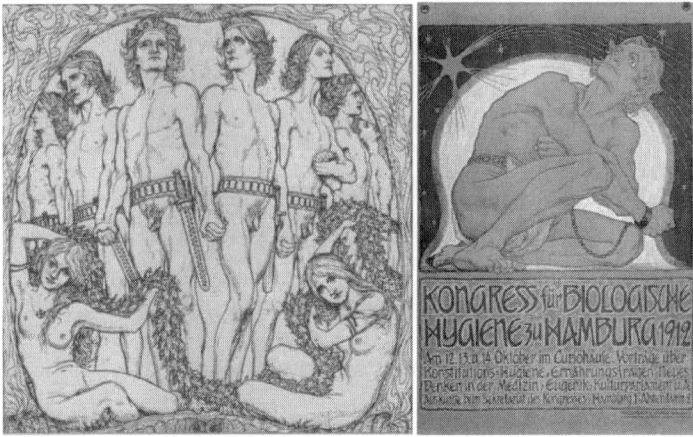

Hugo Reinhold Karl Johann Höppener, known under his pseudonym Fidus (1851 – 1913) was a painter and publisher. He was given the name Fidus, Faithful, because he took the rap for the artist Karl Wilhelm Diefenbach in a nudity scandal concerning a Diefenbach commune outside Munich. Diefenbach encouraged vegetarianism and spurned religion and monogamy. He ended his life among his admirers on Capri. Fidus contributed many of his works to *Der Eigene*. He was devoted to both Art Nouveau and to German mythology. Two of his pictures shown here are *Man Breaking his Chains* and *Rising to the Stars*. He was rediscovered in the 1960s, especially amidst San Francisco hippies. His work can be found in the Berlinishe Galerie and the Jack Daulton Collection in California.

POSTSCRIPT

The paradox for Hitler and company was that their very existence depended on their armed forces, and the foundation of those forces was male bonding. Quite incredibly, the Nazis seemed to never have doubted, for a second, the susceptibility of all German males to homoerotic seduction. Their fear was that it could become an epidemic, a chain reaction, one man homosexually bonding with another, exponentially multiplying into a force of men who would die one for the other, a force capable of annihilating the existing power, as the 300 of Thermopylae had nearly halted the progression of Xerxes, as the Sacred Band had destroyed the Spartans, as Alexander the Great and his faithful followers had conquered the world. Hitler could not take the chance of losing his hold over a brotherhood of men that could sweep him away like a tidal wave, a tsunami awaiting only the man who would break him in two, a new Bismarck, an aspiring Frederick the Great. For such were the Prussians since the beginning of time, an invincible power awaiting the next Thor. He therefore massacred those visible, like Ernst Rhöm. Not because they were homosexual--that seed was in each and every German, he felt--but because they had to be deprived of the compost that would see them spring to life, dragons' teeth that Nietzsche knew were being sown, of whom we have not seen the last.

SOURCES

(1) See my book *John (Jack) Nicholson.*
(2) See my book *Homosexual Warriors.*
(3) See my book *Greek Homosexuality.*
(4) See my book *Gay Genius.*
(5) See my book *Henry III.*
(6) See my book *Hadrian and Antinous.*
(7) See my book *SPARTA.*
(8) See my book *THE SACRED BAND.*
(9) See my book *Boarding School Homosexuality.*
(10) See my book *Renaissance Homosexuality.*
(11) See my book *The Essence of Being Gay.*
(12) See my biography *Michael Hone.*
(13) See my book *Cesare Borgia.*
(14) See my book *Homoerotic Art.*

Abbott Jacob, *History of Pyrrhus*, 2009.
Ady, Cecilia, *A History of Milan under the Sforza*, 1907.
Aldrich and Wotherspoon, *Who's Who in Gay and Lesbian History*, 2001.
Aristophanes, Bantam Drama, 1962.
Aronson, Marc, *Sir Walter Ralegh*, 2000.
Baglione, *Caravaggio*, circa 1600.
Baker Simon, *Ancient Rome*, 2006.
Barber, Richard, *The Devil's Crown--Henry II and Sons*, 1978.
Barber, Stanley, *Alexandros*, 2010.
Beachy, Robert, *Gay Berlin*, 2014. Marvelous.
Bergreen, Laurence, *Over the Edge of the World. Magellan.* 2003.
Bicheno, Hugh, *Vendetta*, 2007.
Bierman, John, *Dark Safari, Henry Morton Stanley*, 1990.
Bury and Meiggs, *A History of Greece*, 1975.
Calimach, Andrew, *Lover's Legends*, 2002.
Carroll, Stuart, *Maryrs & Murderers, The Guise Family*, 2009.
Carry Peter, *True History of the Kelly Gang*, 2000.
Cawthorne, Nigel, *Sex Lives of the Popes*, 1996.
Cellini, Benvenuto, *The Autobiography of Benvenuto Cellini.*
Ceram, C.W., *Gods, Graves and Scholars*, 1951.
Chamberlin, E.R. *The Fall of the House of Borgia*, 1974.
Clark, Christopher, *Iron Kingdom*, 2006.

Cloulas, Ivan, *The Borgia*, 1989.

Cooper, John, *The Queen's Agent*, 2011.

Crompton, Louis, *Byron and Greek Love*, 1985.

Crompton, Louis, *Homosexuality and Civilization*, 2003.

Crowley, Roger, *Empires of the Sea*, 2008. Marvelous.

Curtis Cate, *Friedrich Nietzsche*, 2002.

Davidson, James, *Courtesans and Fishcakes*, 1998.

Davidson, James, *The Greeks and Greek Love*, 2007.

Davis, John Paul, *The Gothic King, Henry III*, 2013.

Defored, Frank, *Big Bill Tilden*, 1975.

Dover K.J. *Greek Homosexuality*, 1978.

Eisler, Benita, *BYRON Child of Passion, Fool of Fame*, 2000. Wonderful.

Erlanger, Philippe, *The King's Minion*, 1901.

Everitt Anthony, *Augustus*, 2006.

Everitt Anthony, *Cicero*, 2001.

Everitt, Anthony, *Hadrian*, 2009.

Fagles, Robert, *The Iliad*, 1990.

Forellino, Antonio, *Michelangelo*, 2005. Beautiful reproductions.

Fothergill, Brian, *Beckford of Fonthill*, 1979.

Frieda, Leonie, *Catherine de Medici*, 2003. Wonderful.

Gayford, Martin, *Michelangelo*, 2013. A beautiful book.

Gillingham, John, *Richard the Lionheart*, 1978.

Goldsworthy Adrian, *Caesar*, 2006

Goldsworthy Adrian, *The Fall of Carthage*, 2000.

Goodman Rob and Soni Jimmy, *Rome's Last Citizen*, 2012.

Goodwin, Robert, *SPAIN*, 2015.

Graham-Dixon, Andrew, *Caravaggio* 2010. Fabulous.

Grant Michael, *History of Rome*, 1978.

Graves, Robert, *Greek Myths*, 1955.

Grazia, Sebastian de, *Machiavelli in Hell*, 1989.

Guicciardini, *Storie fiorentine (History of Florence)*, 1509. Essential.

Halperin David M. *One Hundred Years of Homosexuality*, 1990.

Harris Robert, *Imperium*, 2006.

Herodotus, *The Histories*, Penguin Classics.

Hesiod and Theognis, Penguin Classics, 1973.

Hibbert, Christopher, *Florence, the Biography of a City*, 1993.

Hibbert, Christopher, *The Borgias and Their Enemies*, 2009.

Hibbert, Christopher, *The Great Mutiny India 1857*, 1978. Fabulous.

Hibbert, Christopher, *The Rise and Fall of the House of Medici*, 1974.

Hicks, Michael, *Richard III*, 2000.

Hine, Daryl, *Puerilities*, 2001.

Hochschild, Adam, *King Leopold's Ghost*, 1999.

Hughes, Robert, *The Fatal Shore*, 1987.

Lacey, Robert, *Henry VIII*, 1972.
Lacy, Robert, *Sir Walter Ralegh*, 1973.
Lambert, Gilles *Caravaggio*, 2007.
Landucci, Luca, *A Florentine Diary*, around 1500, a vital source.
Levy, Buddy, *Conquistador*, 2009.
Lévy, *Edmond, Sparte, 1979.*
Lewis, Bernard, *The Assassins*, 1967.
Livy, *Rome and the Mediterranean*
Livy, *The War with Hannibal.*
Lubkin, Gregory, *A Renaissance Court*, 1994.
Lyons, Mathew, *The Favourite*, 2011.
Mallett, Michael and Christine Shaw, *The Italian Wars 1494-1559.*
Malye, Jean, *La Véritable Histore d'Alcibiade*, 2009.
Manchester, William, *A World Lit Only By Fire*, 1993.
Mitford, Nancy, *Frederick the Great*, 1970.
Moore Lucy, *Amphibious Thing*, 2000.
Moote, Lloyd, *Louis XIII, The Just*, 1989.
Mortimer, Ian, 1415, *Henry V's Year of Glory*, 2009.
Nicholl, Charles, *The Reckoning*, 2002.
Noel, Gerard, *The Renaissance Popes*, 2006.
Oosterhuis and Kennedy, *Homosexuality and Male Bonding*, 1991.
Opper Thorsten, *Hadrian*, 2008.
Opper, Thorsten, *Hadrian, Empire and Conflict*, 2008.
Parker, Derek, *Cellini*, 2003, the book is beautifully written.
Pascal, Jean Claude, *L'Amant du Roi*, 1991.
Payne, Robert and Nihita Romanoff, *Ivan the Terrible*, 2002.
Pernot, Michel, *Henri III*, Le Roi Décrié, 2013, Excellent book.
Petitfils, Jean-Christian, *Louis XIII*, 2008, wonderful.
Peyrefitte, Roger, *Alexandre*, 1979.
Plutarch's Lives, Modern Library.
Pollard, .J., *Warwick the Kingmaker*, 2007.
Polybius, *The Histories.*
Rocke, Michael, *Forbidden Friendships*, 1996. Fabulous/indispensible.
Ross, Charles, *Richard III*, 1981.
Rouse, W.H.D., Homer's *The Iliad*, 1938.
Ruggiero, Guido, *The Boundaries of Eros*, 1985.
Sabatini, Rafael, *The Life of Cesare Borgia*, 1920.
Saint Bris, Gonzague, *Henri IV*, 2009.
Saslow, James, *Ganymede in the Renaissance*, 1986.
Seward, Desmond, *Caravaggio – A Passionate Life*, 1998.
Sharaf, Myron, *Fury on Earth: A Biography of Wilhelm Reich*, 1983.
Simonetta, Marcello, *The Montefeltro Conspiracy*, 2008. Wonderful.
Skidmore, Chris, *Death and the Virgin*, 2010.

Skidmore, *Death and the Virgin*, 2007.

Solnon, Jean-Fançois, *Henry III*, 1996.

Stewart, Alan, *The Cradle King, A Life of James VI & I*, 2003.

Stirling, Stuart, *Pizarro Conqueror of the Inca*, 2005.

Strathern, Paul, *The Medici, Godfathers of the Renaissance*, 2003. Superb.

Strauss Barry, *The Spartacus War*, 2009.

Suetonius, *The Twelve Caesar.s*

Tacitus, *The Annals of Imperial Rome.*

Tacitus, *The Histories.*

Tamagne, Florence, *A History of Homosexuality in Europe*, 2004.

Thucydides, *The Peloponnesian War*, Penguin Classics.

Tibullus, *The Elegies of Tibullus*, translated by Theodore C. Williams

Turner, Ralph, *Eleanor of Aquitaine*, 2009.

Unger Miles, *Magnifico, The Brilliant Life and Violent Times*

Unger, Miles, *Machiavelli*, 2008.

Vasari, We would know next to nothing if it were not for him.

Vernant, Jean-Pierre, *Mortals and Immortals*, 1991.

Virgil, *The Aeneid*, Everyman's Library, Knopf, 1907.

Viroli, Maurizio, *Niccolo's Smile, A Biography of Machiavelli*, 1998.

Ward-Perkins Bryan, *The Fall of Rome*, 2005

Warren, W.L., *Henry II*, 1973.

Weir, Alison, *Eleanor of Aquitaine*, 1999. Weir is a fabulous writer.

Weir, Alison, *Mary, Queen of Scots*, 2003.

Weir, Alison, *The Wars of the Roses*, 1995.

Wheaton James, *Spartacus*, 2011.

Wikipedia: Research today is impossible without the aid of this monument.

Williams Craig A. *Roman Homosexuality*, 2010.

Williams John, *Augustus*, 1972.

Wilson, Derek, *The Uncrowned Kings of England*, 2005.

Wright, Ed, *History's Greatest Scandals*, 2006.

Xenophon, *A History of My Time*s, Penguin Classics.

Xenophon, *The Persian Expedition*, 1949.

All pictures are from Wikipedia.

INDEX

Please note that the page numbers are *passim*. An example, Brandt 76 – 102 means that Brandi is found within these pages, but not necessarily on *every* page.

Cover photo: *Bathers* by Henry Scott Tukes